ISRAEL'S AR

12⁹⁵

ISRAEL'S ARMY

Samuel Katz

Presidio Press ★ Novato, California
THE PRESIDIO POWER SERIES
LANDPOWER #3005

Published by Presidio Press
31 Pamaron Way, Novato CA 94949

Library of Congress Cataloging-in-Publication Data

Katz, Samuel M., 1963–
  Israel's army/Samuel M. Katz.
    p. cm.—(Presidio power series. Landpower; 3005)
  ISBN 0-89141-327-8
  1. Israel—Armed Forces. I. Title. II. Series.
UA853.I8K38   1990
355′.0095694—dc20   89-31935
                                                          CIP

Photo Credits:

IDF Spokesman: 1, 9, 17, 38, 42, 48, 51, 65, 66, 71, 79, 86, 89, 90, 95, 98, 108, 114, 117, 129, 132, 133; Sivan Farag, 23; Michael Giladi, ii-iii, vii, 24, 28, 32–33, 34, 35, 36–37, 39, 40, 43, 47 right, 52, 54, 55, 56, 96, 105, 113; Hagit Goren, 85; Yuval Navon, 123; Yoni Reif, 63; Jonathan Torgovnik, 61, 64, 87, 92, 100 right, 104, 107, 131; Alona Yefet 97; Ariel Yeruzalinsky 102; Tal Yodkovik, ix, 25; Michael Zarfati, i

Bamachane: 3, 4, 5, 8, 13, 29, 30, 53, 57, 68, 75; Natan Alpert, 100 left; Noam Armon, 103; Micha Bar-Am, 69, 72, 76; Hanoch Gutman, 47 left, 49, 59, 60; Uzi Keren, 127, 128, 130 left; Alex Libek, x, 6, 16, 18, 20; Shmuel Rachmani, 109, 120, 122; Gilad Shekmah, 26, 41, 44, 45; Michael Zarfati, 80, 81, 83, 88, 93; Avi Simchoni, 26; Shmuel Rachmani, 126; Yossi Tzevker, 130 right; Michael Zarfati, 84

Samuel M. Katz: 19, 22, 31, 110, 111, 112, 121, 124, 125

Sigalit Katz: 21

Israeli Government Press Office: 11

IDF Archives: 10, 14, 15

Printed by Singapore National Printers Ltd, Coordinated by Palace Press

Contents

ISRAEL

— International boundary
--- Armistice Line
☆ Capital

0 ——— 50 Kilometers
0 ——— 50 Miles

Tyre
Litani River
LEBANON
Nahariya
Akko
GOLAN HEIGHTS
SYRIA
Tiberias
Haifa
Sea of Galilee
Nazareth

Hadera
Netanya
Nablus
Jordan River
Herziliya
WEST BANK
Tel-Aviv Yafo
Ramla
☆ Amman
Mediterranean Sea
Ashdod
Jerusalem ☆
Bethlehem
Ashqelon
Hebron
Dead Sea
GAZA STRIP
Gaza
Rafah
Beersheba
JORDAN
Negev Desert
Dimona
Oron
ISRAEL
Sinai Desert
Nahal Ha'Arava
Mizpe Ramon
EGYPT
Yotvata

Acknowledgments

For all its informal and egalitarian personality, TZAVA HAGANAH L'YISRAEL (the Israel Defense Forces or IDF) is a highly secretive body, especially to an author attempting to write its story. A book of this nature could not have been possible without the help and kindness of a good many people, who deserve my thanks. I wish to offer my most sincere gratitude to Brig. Gen. Ephraim Lapid, the IDF Spokesman, who gave me the opportunity to gather all necessary materials for this work, as well as to Maj. Dvora Takson, who, as always, offered me only kindness and as much help as her IDF Spokesman's Public Relations Unit allowed. I also wish to thank Lt. Col. S. at the Censor's Office for his quick and fair review of the manuscript, and my father-in-law, Nissim Elyakim, who so faithfully scurried back and forth from office to office with my manuscript, applying just enough pressure to untangle the labyrinth of bureaucracy "sometimes" encountered in the IDF.

Yet of all the people who have helped me, it was the photographers at the IDF Spokesman, and the IDF's weekly magazine, BAMACHANE, who deserve a special word of thanks. Yuval Navon, Miki Zarfati, the always happy and smiling Rinat Cohen, Jonathan Torgovnik, Michael Giladi, Hagit Goren, Sivan Farag', Tal Yodkovik, Yair Domb, and Ariel Yerozolimski are all highly talented photographers and archivists. They were extremely professional and were kind to me, a person out of the blue who intruded on their day-to-day routines. Last but not least, I wish to offer a heartfelt thanks to my lovely wife, Sigalit, whose love, patience, and ability to cope with a frantic author really made this book possible.

Glossary

AGA'M Acronym for AGAF MIVTZA'IM, the "Operations Branch" of the General Staff. Also used as the title for the combat segment of the officers' course for the Armored Corps, Artillery Corps, Air Defense Unit, and Combat Engineers.

A'MAN Acronym for AGAF MODE'IN, the "Intelligence Branch" of the General Staff.

BA'HAD 1 Acronym for BEIT SEFER L'HADRACHA 1 (Instructional School), the instructional base where Israeli officers are trained.

BAMACHANE The IDF weekly magazine published by the Educational Corps and issued to all Israeli military, police, and Border Guard units.

BARAK Hebrew for lightning. A popular unit designation for armor and infantry units.

CHEN (HEN) Acronym for HEYL NASHIM, the Women's Corps, and also the Hebrew word for "charm."

GAD'NA Acronym for the GDUDEI NO'AR, the Youth Battalions that originated during the struggle for Israeli independence. Once or twice during high school, Israeli teenagers are introduced to the IDF through a week of lectures, and the minimum of para-military and fire-arms training.

GALEI TZAHAL The IDF radio station (literally "IDF Airwaves"), which provides entertainment, news, and educational programming.

GIBUSH The Hebrew for "to unify," but used in military slang for the test period lasting between one day to a week where candidates for elite units, pilots' course, and naval service are examined.

GIVA'ATI Hebrew for "my valley," and the name of an elite infantry division famous for its service in southern Israel during the 1948 War. Reborn in 1984 as a marine-type force, the GIVA'ATI Brigade is today considered one of the IDF's premier infantry units, with a distinguished combat record in southern Lebanon and along Israel's northern frontier.

GOLANI The 1st GOLANI ("my Golan") Brigade was literally the first regular HAGANAH infantry formation. It fought in northern Israel in 1948, in the Sinai desert in 1956, and finally earned its elite rank for the heroic capture of the Golan Heights in 1967. Its subsequent and epic defense of the Golan Heights during the 1973 War elevated the brigade to national heroes.

HAGANAH Pre-independence Israel's popular army, and the IDF's forebear.

HANDASAH KRAVIT Combat Engineers.

HEYL HANDASAH Engineering Corps.

HEYL HAVIR Air Force.

HEYL HAYAM Navy.

HEYL HINUCH Educational Corps.

HEYL KESHER Communications Corps.

HEYL MODE'IN Intelligence Corps.

HEYL RAGLIM Infantry.

HEYL REFUA Medical Corps.

HEYL SHIRION Armored Corps.

HEYL TOTHANIM Artillery Corps.

HIBA Acronym for HAYELOT BE'SHERUT HAMISHTERA (female soldiers in police service), and also the Hebrew word for "affection."

IRGUN Abbreviation for IRGUN TZVAI LEUMI (National Army Organization), the controversial pre-independence underground commanded by Menachem Begin.

KABA Acronym for "quality category score," a psychological testing procedure given to new recruits which reflects an individual's intelligence level, educational level, mastery of the Hebrew language, and projected adjustment to combat service.

KITA Class or squad.

KOURS MAK'IM KOURS MEFAKED KITA, "squad leaders course."

MAF'HA'SH Acronym for MIFKEDET HEYLOT SADEH, the Ground Forces Command.

MASA'A MESAKEM The long forced march which is

endured at the close of basic training, the successful completion of which serves as a prerequisite for graduation.

MATEH HAKLALI General Staff.

MISHTERA TZVA'IT Military Police.

NA'HA'L Acronym for NOAR HALUTZEI LOHEM, the Fighting Pioneer Youth.

PAL'MACH Acronym for PLUGOT MAHATZ, "Strike Companies"; the HAGANAH's elite commando force organized by the British to fight a guerrilla war against the Germans should they have reached Palestine, but instrumental in the following fight against the British and Arabs for Israeli independence.

RA'MAT'KAL Acronym for ROSH MATEH HAKLALI (Chief of Staff), a position held by a lieutenant general.

SA'AR Hebrew for "storm," a popular designation for armor units.

SAYERET Reconnaissance force.

SHILUV KOHOT The IDF's battle doctrine of "combined arms."

SHIN BET (SHERUT BITAHON HAKLALI) Abbreviated name for the General Security Services, Israel's counter-espionage internal security agency (similar in role and mission to the American FBI and Britain's MI5).

TIRONUT Basic training.

TZAHAL Acronym for TZAVA HAGANAII L'YISRAEL or Israel Defense Forces (IDF).

TZA'MA'P Acronym for TZEVET (crew), MAHLAKA (platoon), and PLUGAH (company). The training cycle for tank soldiers fresh out of basic training.

TZANHAN (TZANHANIM pl.) Paratrooper.

Chief of Staff Lt. Gen. Dan Shomron (sun glasses and helmet) is briefed on the newest antitank weapon: the Israel Military Industries B-300.

Prologue

Memorial Day in Israel is an astounding testament to sacrifice and grief. At 11 A.M. the sounds of sirens are heard throughout the land, and in an act of national unison, all Israelis stop in their tracks. They stand at attention in sorrow and awe for two minutes, honoring the more than 15,000 Israeli soldiers killed in the past forty years' seven wars, and the civilian victims of terrorism. Drivers get out of their vehicles, mothers stop strolling their children, and soldiers contemplate their fallen brothers in arms, while at the same time giving a quick thought to their precarious situation as combatants. The only place where the sirens have little meaning is along Israel's frontiers, where the business of safeguarding the state goes on as usual.

The weeping of Memorial Day passes into night, and the joy and celebration of Independence Day begins. Whereas only hours earlier Israelis stood silently in salute to those who sacrificed their lives, they now find themselves in jubilant rejoicing, dancing in the street, singing national songs, and watching fireworks demonstrations. Once again, the young conscripts and graying reservists patrolling the frontiers have little time from their vigilant watch to celebrate another year of statehood.

Remembrance and vigilance are perhaps the best words to describe the Israel Defense Forces and its role in everyday Israeli life. For the past forty years, the TZAVA HAGANAH L'YISRAEL (Hebrew for Israel Defense Forces, best known by the abbreviation IDF) has been the one factor that has allowed the state of Israel to survive within the most secure boundaries possible in the forever volatile Middle East. Although service in the IDF might not be the most glamorous or financially rewarding in the world, it is necessary and essential. From the five-nation Arab invasion of 1948 to the frequent attempts by terrorists to seize hostages along Israel's northern frontier, the poorly paid and casually dressed men and women of the IDF have fought, survived, and triumphed.

STOP: Border Ahead. No Crossing by Command! A sign on the Jordan River, which separates Israel and Jordan.

During the height of Shiite and Palestinian guerrilla activity in southern Lebanon, an IDF M113 passes carefully through the Lebanese cedars on patrol.

Recently, Israel's Army has received a great deal of negative media attention. Because of the Army's show of force in attempting to quell the Palestinians' *intifadah* or ''uprising'' on the West Bank and Gaza Strip, Western newsmen, and as a result much of the world, have begun to view the Israeli soldier as an often brutal occupier. The scenes screened nightly of young paratroopers in their red berets beating Palestinian youths with clubs, and firing tear gas and rubber bullets at women and children, have labeled the once ''holier than thou'' IDF as a harsh military machine. This is perhaps one of the great injustices done to the Israeli soldier. Few armies, especially in the Arab Middle East, can boast the high morale and humane standards displayed by the Israeli soldier.

The Israeli soldier is not, as myth will have it, a superhuman fighter, nor is he a vicious warrior. He is merely a simple soldier produced by a tragically violent history. The IDF's beginnings are humble. It was born out of Israel's pre-independence Jewish underground, the HAGANAH, on 31 May 1948. It was a ragtag army with few uniforms, few weapons, and even fewer chances for victory. Its apparent weakness was clearly one of the factors that prompted the Arab states of Egypt, Transjordan, Syria, Iraq, and Lebanon to invade the infant state a day following its declaration of independence. Yet what the Jewish fighters lacked in hardware they more than made up for in determination, and that very Israeli talent of maximizing meager resources.

With survival at stake, almost every citizen able to carry a gun joined the newly formed IDF. This included the legendary veterans from the PAL'MACH, the British-sponsored commandos formed to fight off a German assault on Palestine, as well as recent arrivals from the ashes of Jewish Europe. It included British WW II veterans, and teenage girls taught the art of demolition. The dire necessity for calling everyone to arms produced a unique spirit of egalitarianism in the IDF, giving it a ''laid back'' personality as well as its members an ability to rally together. In 1948, it was indeed these qualities that allowed the IDF to not only survive eight months of fierce combat but win an astounding victory. The cost of victory was staggering; 6,000 Israeli combatants and civilians were killed, more than 1 percent of the total population. The stiff human price would forever influence Israeli battlefield strategy.

Victory did not bring peace, and the IDF remained a principal element of Israeli life. When hundreds of thousands of Jews the world over came to settle the newly formed Jewish state, the IDF accepted the role not only of nation defender but of nation builder. The IDF helped assimilate these newcomers, providing medical care and teaching Hebrew. It became the largest educational system and cultural institution in Israel. National service laws conscripting both men and women, rich and poor, were intended to make the IDF the one national experience each citizen could truly share.

Following the 1948 War, the IDF was able to procure badly needed weapons and ammunition, but could not achieve peace. The Arab states refused to accept the reality of the state of Israel, and open hostilities continued. In 1952, there were more than 3,000 incidents of Arab infiltrators who crossed into Israel and killed civilians and soldiers at will. The IDF response was a ''small fist with a hefty punch.'' Under the command of a boisterous major named ''Arik'' Sharon, a small retaliatory commando force was formed. Called ''Unit 101,'' it was the budding IDF's first elite fighting formation. Although it never numbered more than forty fighters, Unit 101 attracted the best Israel had to offer, and under the eccentric guidance of Major Sharon, the men were taught to hit hard, hit fast, and give no quarter. They conducted dozens of retaliatory raids deep into Jordanian, Lebanese, and Egyptian territory, often inflicting more fear than damage. They nevertheless became instant celebrities, and 101 became a role model to which other units in the IDF could aspire.

Unit 101 was disbanded after only six months of

active service because of its controversial commander and his methods, but a fledgling paratroop battalion was quick to fill the vacant position. With Arab *fedayeen* attacks increasing in scope and ferocity, the paratroop battalion, which expanded to a brigade, hit the terror bases with daring and inspiring raids. Egypt's sponsoring of the *fedayeen* bands from Gaza proved to be the *casus belli* for an Israeli invasion of Nasser's Egypt in October 1956, carried out in full coordination with the British and French assault on the Suez Canal. Although by today's standards Israel was militarily lacking, the paratroopers did make their legendary

War in Lebanon! An M113 APC loaded with paratroopers lands just north of Sidon on the morning of June 7th, 1982. It was the IDF's largest amphibious operation.

jump behind enemy lines at the Mitla Pass, and the armor vanguard reached the Suez in less than a hundred hours. The IDF had scored its second decisive victory in eight years.

Once again victory did not bring peace, and the seeds for the next conflict were sown. The thirst for Arab retribution following the 1948 and 1956 thrash-

"Returning an old debt." Captured Palestinian BM-21 Katyusha launchers pressed into Artillery Corps service pound Beirut.

ings, compounded with the emergence of a Palestinian guerrilla movement called the Palestine Liberation Organization (PLO), insured that hostilities would continue. But where and when?

The next major confrontation took place on 7 April 1967. In an aerial dogfight above the Golan Heights, a flight of Israeli Air Force (IAF) Mirage IIICs destroyed six Syrian MiGs. Responding to the call for Arab unity, Egyptian President Nasser flexed his muscle by blockading the strategic Red Sea Straits of Tiran. He not only ordered out the United Nations Peacekeeping Force in Sinai, a relic from the 1956 War, but ordered in his Russian-equipped armored divisions! Nasser called upon his Arab brethren to push the infidel Jewish state into the sea; he was answered by war cries from Syria and permission to have the professional Jordanian military placed under overall Egyptian command. In Israel, the reservists, the backbone of Israeli defensive strategy, were called

up and mobilized, while trenches were dug in Tel Aviv. Israel's hour was at hand.

On 5 June 1967 at 0745, while Egyptian commanders ate breakfast, IAF jets attacked almost every Egyptian Air Force base, destroying more than 350 MiGs and Sukhois on the ground. The Egyptian Air Force ceased to exist in a matter of hours, and without any air support, the Egyptian Army amassed in Sinai lay at the mercy of three IDF armored divisions who punched across the southern frontier. The IDF "did unto the Egyptians before it could be done unto them," and the Israeli juggernaut reached the Suez Canal in less than a hundred hours. The Jordanians, who were spared the initial IDF aerial preemptive blitz, fired upon Israeli positions in the divided city of Jerusalem. The IDF responded by pushing into the Jordanian-occupied West Bank, and thus inherited the problem of almost a million Palestinian refugees. In perhaps the most symbolic and historic Middle East military action in 2,000 years, paratroop reservists, many veterans of the 1948 and 1956 wars, recaptured and unified the holy city of Jerusalem. The hardest nut to crack was saved for last, and on 9 June, IDF armor led by the elite GOLANI Infantry Brigade stormed Syria's strategic Golan Heights, which were tenaciously defended by a series of impregnable fortresses. For years, Syrian artillery had shelled the dozens of Israeli agricultural settlements with impunity, but in two days, Israel ended the shellings, and the war. The Middle East would never be the same.

Israel's stunning victory was awe inspiring. The Six Day War had not only seen Israel quadruple her territory, but shatter Arab military might. The Arabs rejected coming to terms with Israel, however, and supported by massive doses of Soviet aid, vowed to regain their lost pride. Before the dust could settle on the battlefields of Sinai and the Jordan Valley, a new outbreak of hostilities commenced. Called the War of Attrition or 1,000 Days War, Egypt, Jordan, and Syria traded artillery and aerial duels with Israeli forces from 1967 to 1970. It was siege warfare meant

4

to take as high a toll as possible in Israeli civilian and military casualties; but Israel dug in, and with hundreds of spectacular commando operations deep into enemy territory, beat the Arabs into submission.

The War of Attrition never really ended, but continued in bloody fashion with the introduction of Palestinian terrorism worldwide. The 130mm cannons were replaced by the hijacker, as the world became the stage for the Middle East madness. Serving biblical justice to the perpetrators of such Palestinian terror outrages as the Lod Airport and Munich Olympic massacres in 1972 became something of an Israeli military obsession. Its intelligence community allowed terrorism to overshadow a still very existing threat — the combined armies of Syria, Jordan, and Egypt. Overconfident by its six days of glory in June 1967, the IDF became a sleeping giant, only to be awakened, as if in a message from the almighty, on Judaism's day of atonement — Yom Kippur.

6 October 1973: Yom Kippur Day. While all of Israel was deep in prayer, the unholy sounds of transport vehicles and jet aircraft were heard throughout the land. Summoned by word of mouth, hundreds of thousands of reservists frantically raced toward the Syrian and Egyptian frontiers to reach their battalions, brigades, and divisions. At 1415, an unprecedented joint Syrian and Egyptian onslaught caught the too few conscript units along the borders *badly* by surprise. Another Israeli day of judgment had arrived.

On the Golan Heights, Syrian surface-to-air missiles (SAMs) succeeded in neutralizing the invincible IAF. Syrian mechanized and armor columns almost succeeded in retaking the Heights, and would have, were it not for the infamous 7th Armored Brigade's stand to the death in the epic ''Valley of Tears,'' and a hell of a lot of luck! Reinforced by the mobilized reservists, the IDF eventually pushed the Syrians not only out of the Golan plateau, but to within artillery range of Damascus.

On the Sinai front, the Egyptians had ingeniously

Dramatic view of ex-PLO Katyushas being launched against the heart of the PLO kingdom in West Beirut: August 1982.

crossed the formidable Suez Canal barrier and captured almost all of the poorly defended Bar-Lev Line strongholds. Aided by a SAM umbrella denser than the one experienced by American pilots over North Vietnam, the Egyptians were able to blast dozens of IAF warplanes out of the sky, while capitalizing on disarray in the IDF ground effort. On 14 October, the Egyptians launched a bold armored thrust out of their SAM umbrella's range to capture the strategic Sinai passes. This time, however, the IDF had regrouped and was ready. In the ensuing tank battle, the largest in military history since Kursk, the IDF tank gunners regained their posture and momentum, destroying more than two hundred Egyptian T-55s and T-62s, while suffering only six damaged vehicles of their own. It was the war's turning point; within days and after much bitter fighting, the IDF crossed the Suez Canal into Egypt proper. After brilliantly encircling the Egyptian Third Army and cutting off

more than 100,000 men for the kill, the IDF pushed for Cairo. Only pressure from the superpowers and a worldwide nuclear alert thwarted Israel in her decisive though costly victory.

The trauma of the surprise Arab attack, personified by the 2,500 dead in but eighteen days of fighting, shocked Israel into a state of self-doubt and fear. Although the war's outcome had been victorious, the war wasn't a sweeping victory as it had been in 1967. For the first time in IDF history, Israelis were taken prisoner by the hundreds. Political and military soul-searching led to numerous resignations, including Prime Minister Golda Meir, Defense Minister Moshe Dayan, and the IDF Chief of Staff. The army, decimated in the brutal fighting, had to be rebuilt; so did its morale.

The ''1973 Earthquake'' was not Israel's only pressing military crisis. Along the Lebanese frontier, Palestinian terror groups had become more bold and

Responding to reports of a suspected explosive device, a paratroop patrol leaves the security of their heavily armored M113 APCs to engage Shiite *Hizballah* guerrillas in southern Lebanon, March 1985.

bloody in their attacks against Israel. In 1974 alone, the infamous massacres at Ma'alot and Kiryat Shmoneh underscored Israeli vulnerability. In June 1976, when an Air France flight en route from Tel Aviv via Athens to Paris was hijacked to Entebbe by an international lot working for the Palestinians, it appeared as if Israel would have to acquiesce. The IDF, however, had other plans. Under the brilliant command of then Chief Paratroop and Infantry Officer, and current Chief of Staff Lt. Gen. Dan Shomron, a mixed recon paratroop and GOLANI Infantry force flew the 3,600 kilometers to Entebbe, and in ninety minutes rescued 103 Israeli and Jewish hostages. The spectacular raid, named ''Operation Yonatan'' in memory of the raid's killed commander Lt. Col. ''Yoni'' Netanyahu, captured world attention, inspiring three feature motion pictures made of the story. Most importantly, it released the IDF from its post–Yom Kippur War malaise. The innovative IDF, capable of the impossible, was back!

The Lebanon situation and Palestinian terrorism soon developed into the IDF's foremost military objectives. From the early 1970s to 1982, hundreds of cross-border retaliatory and preemptive raids were conducted against the Palestinian ministate in southern Lebanon. In March 1978, the IDF even mounted a mini-invasion of southern Lebanon, "Operation Litani," following a particularly vicious seaborne Palestinian attack north of Tel Aviv, which left thirty-eight dead. Lebanon's chaotic situation was a thorn in Israel's side, which everyone knew would be removed one day by force. When Egypt and Israel signed for peace in 1978, military attention was turned from the giant Egyptian military machine to Lebanon and Syria. All that was needed was the spark.

On 3 June 1982, Israel's ambassador to the United Kingdom was seriously injured by Palestinian gunmen in London. Israel responded with an aerial blitz on Beirut, answered by Palestinian Katyusha bombardments into Galilee. With much of northern Israel held hostage in bomb shelters, the intolerable situation allowed the government to settle the Lebanon thorn once and for all. Thirty thousand Israeli troops, the vanguards of one of the strongest military machines in the world, crossed the northern frontier into Lebanon on 6 June 1982. "Operation Peace for Galilee," and Israel's most politically volatile war, was underway.

Initially, the IDF's war against the Palestinians in Lebanon went well. Advances were good, though fighting against fanatic Palestinian and leftist Lebanese Muslim resistance was bloody. With technical and tactical genius, the IAF executed a surgical strike against fourteen Syrian SAM sites in the Beka'a Valley, while at the same time shooting down eighty-two Syrian MiGs without a single loss to themselves.

A ground war ensued, and after much bitter tank fighting in which the Syrians performed well, the IDF was able to cut off the strategic Beirut-Damascus Highway and lay siege to the Lebanese capital.

Israel's massive siege of Beirut achieved the intended result of expelling more than 14,000 Palestinian fighters from the Lebanese capital, but opened a quagmire from which Israel has yet to remove itself. Instead of being able to pull out of Lebanon after the Palestinian exodus, Israel was forced to remain, following the assassination of Christian President-elect Bashir Gemayel and the resulting chaos. An IDF retreat meant a power vacuum filled by the Palestinians and Syrians, so an IDF occupation, awaiting a political solution, followed. Soon, Israel became the "popular enemy," and found itself in a vicious guerrilla war it was unsuited to fight against fanatical Shiite Muslim and returning Palestinian terrorists. For three years, the IDF fought the shadows and suicide bombers, until its eventual pullout in May 1985. The sanity and clear military objectives the IDF had always maintained in its combat doctrine were of little use in a land that could host the "Sabra and Shatilla" massacres, and Shiite terrorist truck bombings of the U.S. Embassy, the Marine headquarters in Beirut, and the IDF headquarters in Tyre. In Lebanon, the IDF lost more than 700 dead, thousands of wounded, and much of its innocence.

Today, Israel and the IDF face a host of serious threats to their physical existence. From the new long-range missiles and chemical warfare capabilities possessed by the Syrians, to terrorist attacks from across the Lebanese border, to the current *intifadah* on the West Bank and Gaza, Israel finds itself entangled in a labyrinth of war and conflict. Yet while historians will file Israel's past forty years in the context of the Middle East's 2,000-year-history, and while politicians debate and negotiate, the task of the simple soldier remains the same. For the Israeli soldier, history is an incentive to fight hard, fight tough, fight on, and persevere. This is their story.

Chapter 1
The Israel Defense Forces: Order of Battle

The tragic history of the ancient "Children of Israel" serves as very real motivation for modern Israel to do anything within its power to survive. For all its seeming political turmoil and very tangible economic instability, Israel has from day one of its independence mobilized the better portion of its national resources for defense. It has little choice in the matter. Forty years after her declaration of independence, enemies still wish to destroy the state of Israel. Today Israel devotes more than 40 percent of her national budget to the IDF, which boasts a standing Army, Navy, and Air Force of 140,000 conscripts, 50,000 professional soldiers, and an impressive force of 410,000 reservists. Should this potent punch prove incapable of stemming an all-out Arab effort, Israel can further mobilize a remaining 690,000 of its citizens who are deemed capable of military duty. For this nation of only 4 million souls, survival is a national obsession.

Unique among the fanatical dictators and monarchies of the Middle East, command of Israel's military might lies not with the generals of a junta, but in the hands of an elected, civilian government. Overall control lies with the Cabinet, which operates the IDF through the Defense Minister. Administrative and operational control of the IDF is in the hands of the Chief of Staff (RA'MAT'KAL), usually a paratroop officer whose combat leadership skills and past military record are unquestionable. The General Staff (MATEH HAKLALI) is a forum of military commanders in which

---

GOLANI infantrymen make their way past the skeletons of airliners at Beirut International Airport, August 1982.

An armored column of Centurion and M-60 MBTs makes its way through the rubble of the ex-PLO stronghold of Sidon, during the first week of war — June 1982.

the Intelligence and Operations commands are represented — the three territorial commands (Northern, Central, and Southern), as well as the Manpower Branch, Air Force, Navy, and the Ground Forces Command. The Ground Forces Command (MAF-'CHA'SH) is the latest addition to the General Staff and includes overall command of the one conscript and four reserve Paratroop brigades, the GOLANI and GIVA'ATI infantry brigades, the Armored Corps divisions, Artillery Corps, and the Combat Engineers. Other branches of the IDF, including the Women's Corps (CHEN), Military Police, Ordnance, Medical, Education, Rabbinate, Adjutancy, Judge Advocate

With only yards and the Suez Canal separating their position from Egyptian lines, reservists try to catch up on the news they're creating.

General, General Services, and even the conscript NA'HA'L "fighting pioneer youth" infantry units, are under independent though subservient command.

Also quite unique among most armies of the world is the IDF's policy of unifying its different branches of service into a single homogenous command. There is no separate IDF Army, Navy, or Air Force. With the Chief of Staff as the supreme commander of the

IDF in its entirety, the Air Force and Navy are allowed to ''behave'' as distinct ''combat arms'' with their own unique personalities. They are not, however, separate entities. The popular misconception, induced by bad war movies, of sailors, airmen, and grunts battling one another in barroom brawls, fighting solely for unit pride, could never happen in the IDF. Each soldier, from naval radar technician to air crewman to logistics NCO, is considered equal, with each one undergoing an identical ''conscription to release'' life span in his and her military service, no matter what the uniform. Each eighteen-year-old Israeli ''becomes'' an Israeli soldier at BA'K'UM. the IDF's con-

scription depot, and the hapless conscripts undergo a similar progression through the ranks — basic training, a professions course, and for the majority, three years of monotonous though necessary labor with combat boots. The only true differences between sailors, airmen, and ground soldiers are their unique military skills and experiences.

As the IDF is constantly challenged in its declared

A lone Israeli reservist surveys a battalion-strength assortment of Egyptian POWs captured during the Israeli blitzkrieg into Sinai during the 1967 Six Day War.

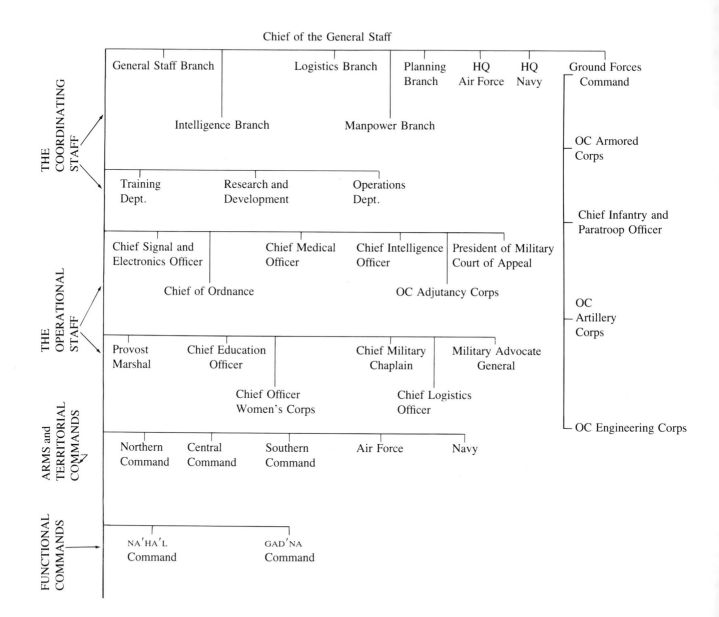

Chief of the General Staff

THE COORDINATING STAFF

General Staff Branch   Logistics Branch   Planning Branch   HQ Air Force   HQ Navy   Ground Forces Command

Intelligence Branch   Manpower Branch

Training Dept.   Research and Development   Operations Dept.

OC Armored Corps

THE OPERATIONAL STAFF

Chief Signal and Electronics Officer   Chief Medical Officer   Chief Intelligence Officer   President of Military Court of Appeal

Chief of Ordnance   OC Adjutancy Corps

Chief Infantry and Paratroop Officer

Provost Marshal   Chief Education Officer   Chief Military Chaplain   Military Advocate General

Chief Officer Women's Corps   Chief Logistics Officer

OC Artillery Corps

ARMS and TERRITORIAL COMMANDS

Northern Command   Central Command   Southern Command   Air Force   Navy

OC Engineering Corps

FUNCTIONAL COMMANDS

NA'HA'L Command   GAD'NA Command

12

Always vigilant, always on alert, always busy as hell! Off the coast of Lebanon, an IDF/Navy DABUR 20mm gunner covers a merchant ship suspected of ferrying Palestinian terrorists to southern Lebanon.

task to defend the state of Israel, its well-equipped and professional Navy, Air Force, and Army are on constant "battle stations," expecting the call to action at every moment. Both the HEYL HAYAM (Navy) and HEYL HAVIR (Air Force) have their own histories — their long lists of dead, wounded, and brave, and their twenty-four-hour-a-day gripping saga of keeping the Arab enemies at bay. But it's the men and women of the Ground Forces Command that are the mainstay of the IDF, the soldiers who sit inside the claustrophobic confines of a MERKAVA MBT (main battle tank), load a 155mm shell into the breech of their self-propelled gun, and patrol a deserted street in southern Lebanon expecting an RPG (rocket-propelled grenade)

"They're back to being their old selves, and we're back to being like we used to be in the old days!" Mechanized IDF reservists pass a destroyed Syrian vehicle on the road to Damascus, 1973.

and burst of AK fire at every second. These are the soldiers who stormed the Old City of Jerusalem in 1967, fought the most brutal tank battle in military history atop the Golan Heights in 1973, and dazzled the world by rescuing 103 of their own in Entebbe. They are the striking punch of the IDF, its true heart and soul.

Although the security-sensitive IDF has never officially released the revealing numbers behind its mighty order of battle, independent reports have listed an impressive IDF "Ground Force Command" arsenal. The IDF has many times been called a tank army, because of its numerous armored divisions (the exact number and designations remaining highly classified) for a first-line ground defense. Its armor juggernaut consists of 3,000 main battle tanks, including more than 2,500 highly upgraded and re-armored Centurions and Pattons, as well as more than 300 MERKAVA Mk. Is and IIs, with an up-gunned Mk. III variant under production. The IDF also has on call more than 500 Russian-made ex-Egyptian, -Syrian, and -PLO T-54/55s and T-62s. Behind the IDF's great tank army is a faithful force of paratroopers, and GOLANI, GIVA'ATI, and NA'HA'L mechanized infantrymen, who are all ferried to the battlefield on the IDF's fleet of more than 4,000 re-armored M113s, as well as captured Arab Soviet BTRs. Providing the fire support for the tanks and infantry are the unheralded gunners of HEYL TOTHANIM, the IDF's Artillery Corps, armed with more than 1,000 batteries of self-propelled firepower, ranging from small- and large-caliber Israeli-produced mortars, to captured Russian 130mm guns, to the big boys — American-made 155mm and 175mm self-propelled guns. HEYL TOTHANIM also deploys a wide assortment of rockets and missiles, including captured Katyushas, which once threatened Israel's northern border, and Lance surface-to-surface missiles.

Yet beyond the numbers, figures, and designations, the IDF's main strength is its human component. The men and women who carry the "blue and white"–produced UZIS and GALILS serve their required years of national service, and then consider themselves on call twenty-four hours a day for a better portion of their future lives.

October 1973. Under heavy Syrian artillery, rocket, and tank fire, a lone Israeli Centurion takes aim into the rolling hills of the Golan Heights.

Chapter 2
Israelis and the IDF: A Marriage of Necessity

The year 1988 was a monumental one for the state of Israel. After seven wars, countless security operations, and hundreds of terrorist attacks, Israel earned the right to celebrate her fortieth anniversary. Making possible the first forty years of "living on the edge" had been the responsibility of the nation's guardians, the TZAVA HAGANAH L'YISRAEL, or the Israel Defense Forces.

The IDF at one time or another will touch the lives of every single Israeli citizen. Since almost every Israeli becomes a soldier (except religious or married women, ultra-orthodox men, and Arabs—although Druze Muslims are conscripted and many Bedouins volunteer!), the IDF is *the* central aspect of Israeli life. At the age of sixteen every Israeli teenager receives a call to take a series of aptitude and psychotechnical examinations in the first step toward military service. Two years later, they exchange the memories of high school for fatigues and kit bags. Most Israelis will meet their best friends while in uniform, as well as fall in love with their future wives and husbands. Since all Israeli men must serve in the reserves until

their fifty-fifth birthday, they will spend an astounding total of *nine* years in uniform.

One might think that such monumental responsibility would create resentment among the Israelis, but it doesn't. In a grudging, and typical, Israeli fashion, a love-hate relationship has existed between citizen and citizen army for the past forty years. The IDF

An honor guard stands at attention beneath a sign reading "You should love the compassionate"!

A squad of paratroopers advances behind the safety of their M113s during the breakthrough at Sidon — scene of some of the most bitter fighting of the 1982 Lebanon War.

has responded in kind, developing into far more than an army.

Since defense and security have always been a life and death issue for Israel, it is not surprising that the IDF would assume a central role in Israeli life. As wave after wave of immigrants reached the shores of the newly created Jewish homeland, it was the IDF that was entrusted with building them homes, teaching them Hebrew, and providing them with medical care. When the immigrants became soldiers, the IDF was entrusted to teach these newcomers what the Israeli experience was all about. In an egalitarian approach to soldiering, eighth-generation sabras and recent arrivals were thrown together in Israel's one truly national experience. As a result, the IDF soon became a powerful military force, but one with a very human face.

Today, the tradition of nation builder continues. With a never-ending stream of new arrivals from lands as diverse as the Soviet Union and Ethiopia, new immigrants conscripted into the IDF are still taught Hebrew by dedicated ''soldier teachers.'' Once Hebrew is mastered, a host of magazines are available to inform the soldiers, ranging from BAMACHANE (''in the base''), the IDF's weekly magazine, which reports army *and* civilian news, to more specialized, in-depth periodicals, such as SKIRA HODSHIT or (''monthly review''), the commissioned officer's journal of international political and military affairs.

Having so much contact with everyday Israeli life allows the IDF to exert a massive cultural influence. Army service, be it in peacetime or during the heat of battle, has been the subject of debate, novels, and song. Soldiers are encouraged to become artistically active, and are even offered discounts on films, theatrical events, and concerts. All of the IDF's combat arms, including the territorial commands, maintain choirs that for years have sung the nation's popular songs. Yet none of these avenues of artistic expression of military service glorify war. In fact the opposite is true, since most army choir songs pray for peace.

Israeli citizens remember the ever present threat of Palestinian terrorism as parents and children visit an eerie museum display of terrorist paraphernalia, including a Katyusha launcher.

The most popular topic to explore is the suffering and loss that war brings to the individual soldier, family, and nation as a whole. From plays depicting maimed veterans to moving songs of peace, the IDF has always attempted to deflect the brutalization that military service can bring into a humane art form.

In its cultural service to the nation, the IDF army radio station is a remarkable phenomenon. Called GALEI TZAHAL or "IDF Airwaves," the station is operated by the Educational Corps; it employs a pop music format and plays everything from Chuck Berry to local songs to heavy metal, all in the hope that it will help relieve military monotony. It has news programs that examine everything from the never-relaxed world of Israeli economics to human interest stories — a recent one focused on a poet who happened to be a MAG gunner in a GOLANI infantry section. The most popular program is hosted by a female disc jockey who speaks to soldiers remaining behind in their barracks on Friday nights while the majority have gone home on leave. It is an *army* station with specific military responsibilities, however, and in one of its most controversial moves, GALEI TZAHAL censored a song called "Shooting and Crying" because of its harsh views of the IDF's show of force in the West Bank and Gaza Strip. Armies after all, even the IDF, have to maintain a delicate political balance.

Politics and the IDF are in fact a contradiction in terms. In a country such as Israel — former Prime Minister Golda Meir perhaps stated the national political atmosphere best when she called her job "a prime minister of 3 million presidents" — political ideology and military service have under strict orders never been mixed, and for good reason. With more than a dozen political parties ranging from right-wing revisionists to Marxists, the Israeli political spectrum does

MPs form up to act as an honor guard for an Independence Day military display.

not afford a cohesive military atmosphere. Politics have little to do with military service: Many of the toughest elite unit commanders are "peacenik" leftists from socialist kibbutzim, and many of the most fervent right-wing hard-liners make sure they will never serve even near front-line units. Nevertheless, under strict General Staff orders, politics are never to be discussed or debated by men in uniform and political favors are not to be sought. Although not an easy undertaking considering the many politically volatile situations the Israeli soldier has been placed in, the IDF abhorrence of combining politics and soldiering has guaranteed that a military junta would never form among officers, that generals would never override law and order, and that political decisions would never be refuted by military might. As many IDF generals have often proudly stated, "removing politics from the IDF has kept us clean!"

A reservist confronts two MPs with an attitude about his slightly non-regulation appearance! Israeli soldiers are often disdainful of military "trappings."

21

This philosophy was severely put to the test by an innocent little training film that became a national sensation. The IDF Spokesman's Office, the IDF's embassy to the outside world, was ordered to come up with a short movie dealing with the difficulty of issuing orders in the madness of the Israeli presence in southern Lebanon. The film was meant for BAHAD 1, the IDF's version of West Point, and was to address all aspects of Israeli command ethics, such as innovation, control, humanity, and of course, adherence to "purity of arms." The actors were all Israeli soldiers and Lebanese civilians, the location was a real southern Lebanese village, and the period of filming included the last Israeli pullback in spring 1985. The final product turned out to be something of a loaded pistol. Instead of teaching officers how to lead, the film questioned many of the political and military

GOLANI infantrymen in a jovial mood, returning home to Tel Aviv from service along the Lebanese border. In Israel the sight of armed soldiers is a part of everyday life.

orders issued to the hapless conscripts during the Lebanon duty. Worse, the film's directors chose as the title *Two Fingers from Sidon,* a direct quote from a false statement made by then Defense Minister Arik Sharon, regarding the limitation of the IDF advance into Lebanon in June 1982. (He had placed two fingers on a large wall map, claiming this would be the extent of the advance, while a thrust toward Beirut was actually planned.) Even though *Two Fingers from Sidon* posed a potent political problem, then Chief of Staff Moshe Levy, in a brave decision, gave the film a green light.

The young officer cadets in BAHAD 1 were moved

by the film, and they demanded that their loved ones also be allowed to view it. Lebanon had much the same effect on Israel that Vietnam had on America, even more so considering that Lebanon borders Israel. Although all Israelis serve in the army, few knew the anguish, confusion, and brutality of serving amid Lebanon's massacres, car-bombers, and chaotic landscape. The young conscripts had borne the brunt of harsh duty in that embittered land for almost three years, and they wanted their family members and friends to realize what they had endured. In a matter of weeks, *Two Fingers from Sidon* was released in cinemas nationwide, and it soon became the most popular film in Israeli history. Mothers wept openly when they saw the depictions of fear, fatigue, and stress that their sons had to contend with daily. To understand the plight of these simple soldiers battling an enemy with no uniform, and the tragic results it produced, became an important cause in many Israeli circles. Perhaps most importantly, the film offered a clear explanation as to why many Lebanon veterans returned depressed and apathetic. Through the frank and open relationship between Israelis and the IDF, the country was able to come to terms with its Lebanon experience while still actually living it.

So when Israel's fortieth anniversary rolled around, Israelis and their alter-ego defense forces joined in a united celebration. On the beautiful sunny morning of 26 April 1988, hundreds of thousands of Israelis filed into a dozen or so IDF bases that were open to the public. Hundreds of walking tours were conducted over the famous battlefields spread throughout the land; from the Golan Heights to the Old City of Jerusalem, civilians were entitled to walk on the same ground where their fellow countrymen had fought and died only a few years back. A museum was even opened that offered for display the thousands of tanks, cannons, and rifles captured from the Arabs in the last forty years of conflict. The climax of the day was a military demonstration held in a huge outdoor stadium just outside of Tel Aviv. It included an impressive

flyover by almost every warplane in the Israel Air Force inventory, followed by a parade representing every IDF unit, and a light and sound show in which forty years of national service were celebrated in song and dance. The finale was meant to remind everyone just exactly why there was an IDF. With the stadium blackened, the sounds of tanks, armored personnel carriers, machine gun fire, and explosions were heard. The current generation of Israeli soldiers demonstrated in clear and decisive fashion just how the next war will be fought, while past and perhaps future generations of combatants looked on in awe. The whole spectacle was televised live so that all Israelis could share in this ceremony of affection between a people and her guardians. Israeli television also reaches Jordan, Syria, and Lebanon, so the display became a poignant reminder of not only why Israel maintains this special relationship with her military but her resolve, and her ability, to use it.

IDF markers in an Israeli cemetery: the ultimate price for service.

Chapter 3
Frontier Duty: The GIVA'ATI Infantry Brigade

Dawn on Israel's border with Lebanon is a tranquil, beguiling time. The spring sun has yet to appear over the eastern horizon, and the hills are covered in a peaceful dawn's haze. The beauty of the plush meadows, eucalyptus trees, and rolling hills almost makes you forget where you are, until you hear the buzz of radio communications and the grinding movement of M113s, and notice the fence. All that separates the north of Israel from Lebanon are a few rows of thickly coiled barbed wire supported by electronic sensory devices. The fence runs along a sixty-three-mile stretch from Rosh Hanikra by the Mediterranean shore to the Syrian border. As a local commander says wryly: "China has her Great Wall, and Israel has its 'fence'!" What makes the fence such an obstacle are the men who patrol it. Along with Border Guard Police professionals, stationed along the Lebanese frontier as part of the joint-security arrangement between the National Police and the IDF, the fence is guarded by the best infantrymen the IDF can field. These soldiers are superbly trained, highly

motivated, seasoned veterans, and all from eighteen to twenty-one years of age. To them, service along the fence is much more than active duty; it's a rite of passage.

Today, the Lebanese border near Syria, known as bandit country, is defended by the young conscripts

Humping it, GIVA'ATI style. An officer, with his trusted radioman never more than a step behind, leads his men through the Lebanese countryside near Israel.

A sea of purple berets. GIVA'ATI infantrymen line up for inspection.

of the GIVA'ATI Infantry Brigade. Since its rebirth in 1984, the GIVA'ATI Infantry Brigade has done more than its share to prove its combat worth. Originally intended to be the IDF's amphibious strike force much like the U.S. Marines, the brigade has rapidly advanced into the IDF's premier infantry brigade. Through hard work, harsh training, and persistent commanders, the GIVA'ATI Brigade began raising eyebrows by beating elite paratroop and GOLANI units during interservice exercises. They distinguished themselves to such a point that Southern Command, the brigade's patron saint, pushed for it to be issued a distinctive GIVA'ATI purple beret. Yet even though they were formed for amphibious warfare and belong

to Southern Command, GIVA'ATI has done its best work way up north, along the fence.

Near the fence, GIVA'ATI's bright purple berets are not to be seen. Class A uniforms have been replaced by poor-fitting fatigues, flak vests, web gear, Kevlar ballistic helmets, and of course the soldier's personal weapon. All along the border, no one goes anywhere or does anything without a GALIL rifle slung across the back. When eating at the mess, buying a pack

At a forward firing base somewhere within the 12-kilometer-wide security belt inside southern Lebanon, a GIVA'ATI rifleman aims his GALIL at a suspicious vehicle passing dangerously near the base perimeter.

of cigarettes at the canteen, or visiting the latrine, the weapon is always at hand. The soldier's best friend, the GALIL is an example of Israeli genius. A cross between the AK-47 and the M-16, the 5.56mm GALIL is a sturdy piece of reliability. It can be field-stripped in a matter of seconds, can fire in all climate conditions, wet and covered with mud, and the long-barreled version has a built-in bipod and barbed-wire cutter. The infantryman cares for it, sleeps with it, and knows it is what will keep him alive in a firefight.

The thought of a firefight is always on an infantry-man's mind along the fence, especially when he's awakened for dawn patrol. Dawn patrol is the hardest of all, for this is the terrorists' favorite time for at-tempting a border crossing. The blurry light and dense haze are ideal cover for the terrorists, whereas the IDF soldiers may be sluggish, with red eyes and slow trigger fingers. Yet no matter how the soldiers might hate getting up that early for a six-hour ride along the fence, the consequences of a successful terrorist crossing are very real and provide good motivation. The border is dotted with dozens of towns and agricul-tural settlements such as Ma'alot and Misgav Am, whose names are now synonymous with terrorist mas-sacres. The inhabitants of these places, just a twenty-minute hike from the fence, are totally dependent on these young infantrymen for their physical safety. The soldiers are also detemined not to allow any terror-ist attacks to come down during *their* patrols. As Second Lieutenant Rami, a nineteen-year-old GIVA'ATI officer who already has dozens of Lebanon forays under his belt, is proud to comment: ''We won't let one murderer past us!''

For the soldiers guarding the line, anxiety and stress are a way of life. The men relieve their frustrations through chain-smoking, eating tons of sunflower seeds, cleaning weapons, and reading. Per capita, Israelis are the most avid readers in the world, and many soldiers, especially the GIVA'ATI riflemen, find themselves with little else to do with their free time. They read up on current events or look at automobile magazines, dreaming of the Ferraris they'll never own. What is blatantly absent from their libraries are stories on war. With almost every spot in the nation a memo-rial to fallen war dead, and with almost every citizen in uniform at one time or another, these young men don't have to read others' accounts of battlefield glory or horror to know what war is like. They live on one of the most volatile front lines in the world.

The only communal form of release is watching the nightly news on television at 2100. All soldiers not on patrol, from battalion commanders to simple riflemen just out of basic training, sit around a spartan recreation room, decorated with thin coats of army paint and filled with thick clouds of cigarette smoke. The news is upsetting, as is usually the case in Israel, and hits close to home. The first news item is on the Palestinian rioting in the Balata Refugee Camp in Nablus; the report raises the morale of the men, since this unit just finished a long stretch amid the rubber bullets, stones, and misery of the Gaza Strip, and they are relieved to be anywhere else on this earth, even along this fence in Lebanon. The smiles soon fade as the following story turns to their territory. The anchorman's report on Shiite *Hizballah* terrorists aiding Palestinian attempts to infiltrate into Israel re-sults in an astounding silence throughout the room. Realizing how precarious their situation is, many of the men decide it's about time to get some sleep. After all, those Palestinian and Lebanese faces seen via satellite on television just might be on the other side of the fence during the next patrol.

Sleep time is short, and wake-up is instantaneous. The GIVA'ATI infantrymen have all slept in full uni-form, and each soldier knows that the platoon com-mander will not tolerate laziness. More importantly perhaps, squad members are quite particular about serving with a man unwilling to do his share; if the squad sergeant's wake-up ''kiss'' isn't enough to get a sluggard out of bed, peer pressure most definitely is. Following a quick breakfast of white cheese, olives, and ''what appears to be bread,'' the patrols make

A GIVA'ATI officer guides his men through an "urban combat obstacle course." Skills learned will help them survive the next mission to a Palestinian-held city, or a *Hizballah* HQ.

their way to the briefing. With the exception of a quick trigger finger, the briefing is the most crucial aspect of the patrol. The platoon is given the latest intelligence, weather information, and deployment scenarios in case of engagement. It is crucial to know one's backup, be it a mechanized GOLANI force a few kilometers away, or airborne artillery — Bell 209 Cobra and Hughes Defender helicopter gunships. Canteens are then filled to capacity, insuring that no sloshing sounds give away positions, and a final weapons check is conducted. As the men exit their base for the patrol, a nervous battalion operations officer offers words of reassurance.

Although security considerations forbid giving the exact location of the patrol this April morning, it can be said that it is somewhere near Mount Dov, a geographical elevation performing the duty of junction between Lebanon, Syria, and Israel. Mount Dov wasn't its original name, but commemorates an Israeli soldier killed there while in pursuit of Palestinian guerrillas years back. Most of the GIVA'ATI riflemen don't know Dov's story, but they know what a Lebanese mountain named after an IDF soldier stands for. Mount Dov is a hotbed of terrorist activity, and has been for the past twenty years. Between 1968 and 1972, Mount Dov was an incessant battlefield between Palestinian guerrillas and the IDF. The Lebanese side of Mount Dov along the foothills to Mount Hermon in the northeast became known as ''Fatahland,'' a reference to the virtual exclusive control of the area by the PLO's military arm, *el-Fatah*. The battles fought were harsh, and often at close range. The area's deep caves, steep ravines, inhospitable undergrowth, and extreme seasonal climate made it ideal for unconventional warfare and close-quarter firefights. To get to Israel from their terrorist bases in Lebanon's Beka'a Valley, the Palestinian infiltrators must cross positions manned by the pro-Israeli South Lebanese Army (SLA), IDF positions inside the twelve-kilometer-wide security belt, and then the mountain itself. The fact that Mount Dov is still a ''hot zone'' is a testament to the determination of both the Palestinians and the IDF.

A GIVA'ATI sniper readies his M-21 7.62mm sniper's rifle while waiting for unwelcome visitors on the Lebanese side of the border.

The well-publicized fact that in 1987 IDF and Border Guard patrols killed 230 Palestinian terrorists attempting to cross the fence sticks in the mind of each soldier guarding the frontier. Crossings can be detected in the security zone, or after the fact, when one has succeeded. Threats can also come from the sky, as was seen in November 1987, when a determined Palestinian terrorist crossed the border by hang glider and killed six Israeli infantrymen near Kiryat Shmoneh. As a result of what is now known in Israel as the "Night of the Hang Glider," the soldiers tend to raise eyes as well as gun sights during each and every patrol.

All patrols are completely mobile, with grayish sand-colored command cars. These cars, known by the Hebrew acronym BATA'SHIOT, or "joint security vehicles," have been specifically converted to seat six soldiers — a driver, a tracker, and four soldiers who sit in the rear, two on a side, back to back. As the patrol vehicles go back and forth throughout the shift, the setup allows the soldiers on each side to concentrate their gun sights and attention onto enemy territory. In addition, most infantrymen have a dual weapons role, and LAWs (light antitank weapons), M203s, and RPGs are brought along for good measure. The real kick to the party comes from the FN MAG 7.62mm light machine gun fitted with projection lights and plenty of ammo. A number of vehicles conduct each patrol, driving along the sandy curbside adjacent to the fence with the misleading name of KVISH HAMETUSHTASH, best translated as the "cover-up road." The path of thinly sprinkled sand actually is meant to *uncover* every footprint or mark made by infiltrators. While the first vehicle slowly proceeds along the KVISH HAMETUSHTASH, another command car rides shotgun along the paved thoroughfare reserved for military vehicles. They are to provide support fire should detection of a crossing attempt be made.

The KVISH HAMETUSHTASH is perhaps the most impressive feat of the fence, especially because of its reliance on human skill over technology. Although the entire fence is fitted with electronic safeguards, which sound a warning at a master command post each time the fence is touched, the sand path is an even more valuable aid — it shows not only each footprint, but the direction in which it is headed. The fact that the fence can be crossed without touching or cutting it, especially in areas where the Lebanese side is on higher ground, gives the sandy KVISH HAMETUSHTASH special importance. To keep the coat of sand fresh, the lead truck trails a huge ring of barbed wire, which acts as a giant broom sweeping the path smooth time and time again. The man responsible for reading the road is the tracker, an integral and certainly the most vital element of all IDF-Police border security operations. Sitting next to the driver, the Bedouin or Druze Muslim tracker uses his family-taught skills of the desert to detect and interpret each sign on the sand. His eyes are as valuable as a dozen electronic sensors, and his instincts and courage worth more than a dozen riflemen.

National Police Border Guard BATA'SHIT slowly proceeds along a stretch of the "cover-up" road during a patrol along the "fence."

Outside of Israel, little is known of the non-Jewish or minority soldiers in the IDF, but their service is both voluntary and welcomed. Since 1948, thousands of Arabs have fought on the side of Israel. Although the Druze Muslims are the only non-Jews actually conscripted into the IDF, thousands of Bedouins, Circassians, and Arab Christians volunteer to serve alongside their fellow Jewish citizens. There is even an entire brigade made up of Druze and minority soldiers, complete with its own paratroop-trained reconnaissance force or SAYERET. They have fought with distinction in most of Israel's wars and security operations, including Lebanon, where many times they have faced members of their own faiths on the opposite side of the battlefield.

The Bedouin tracker personifies security duty along Israel's frontiers, and Halil is as good as they get. An experienced professional with ten years of service

31

under his belt, Halil has outward mannerisms and a broad smile that give little insight into his expertise. Yet one look into Halil's shrewd and observing eyes uncovers the tracker's secret weapon. From his perch next to the driver, Halil trains his eagle eyes on the sandy road, knowing it like the palm of his hand. Whenever a mark appears in the road, no matter how minuscule, Halil leaps out of his seat, grabs his American M-16, the tracker's favorite weapon, and examines the sand with a shepherd's patience. If he determines the mark to be nothing, Halil marks off the spot with his foot, and the patrol is allowed to proceed. No matter how high ranking an officer is commanding the patrol, operations do not continue without the tracker's okay. Although the battle cry of IDF officers is "follow me," along Israel's frontiers, "follow me" is a tracker exclusivity.

By stopping to examine suspicious marks, the tracker cuts through the monotony and tension of the patrol. A few men are then ordered off the command car, to patrol on foot. Walking the line allows the soldiers to stretch tired limbs, as well as deploy in quick-firing positions should something develop. Aboard the command car, road markers, geographic landmarks, and the yearning for a smoke are the only things that help pass time, except of course for contact.

When the patrol commander receives word that physical contact has been made along the fence, anxiety is replaced with fear, and boredom with adrenaline. The patrols move at intervals that allow them to be just moments from a point of trouble; yet this offers little comfort to the commanding officer, a twenty-three-year-old captain named Asher, who orders his drivers to burn rubber. Although it is too early for weapons to be cocked, every soldier has already clutched his GALIL's magazine, checked his grenades,

When GALIL's and MAGs just aren't enough, the GIVA'ATI fighters serving up north can always count on the black beret comrades in the Armored Corps.

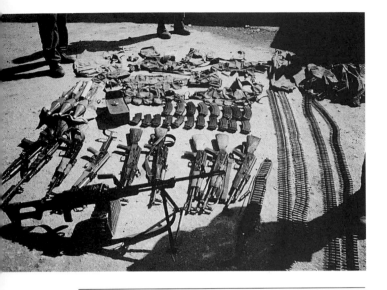

The results of a successful patrol into "peaceful" Lebanon: AK-47s, some even with silencers, RPKs, and RPGs.

and fastened his helmet. The moments of greatest anguish are the few seconds when the tracker jumps off the vehicle to check out the suspect spot. The stopped vehicles make lovely targets inside an RPG's sight. Expecting an ambush, each soldier trains his weapon at ten-meter intervals across the border, especially the "MAGist," whose bursts of 7.62mm light machine gun fire must provide cover to the men sprinting into firing positions. In the end, however, Halil determines the tracks belong to a goat, a straggler looking for food in the wrong place. Halil's skills are such that he can even guess the goat's weight and temperament, but this is of little interest to Captain Asher, who radios in the welcome report to HQ.

From the command car, the patrolling GIVA'ATI soldiers are treated to a host of scenic delights. Through the haze, the lights from the kibbutzim or agricultural communes of Avivim, Kfar Yuval, Yif-

tach, and Misgav Am are visible. Each kibbutz has been the scene of a terrorist incident, a fact that clearly sticks in the minds of the men. On the other side of the fence, the Lebanese countryside fills the imagination. An SLA position, a farmer's tractor, and rolling hills with the first purple flowers of spring. The physical beauty of the area leads the soldiers' minds to wander, and soon the sandy KVISH HAMETUSHTASH resembles a Tel Aviv beach, . . . but the sight of the battalion commander inspecting the patrol in his ex-PLO Chevy Blazer 4x4 brings *everyone* back to reality. There are still two hours remaining on watch!

The eventless end of the patrol is signaled with a sigh of relief. For most of this GIVA'ATI platoon, the end of this journey along the fence means leave. It has been two weeks since the men have seen home, and there are clean beds to sleep in, and home-cooked food to be eaten, and of course girlfriends to see. Upon returning to base, fatigues will be exchanged for Class A's, and dusty helmets replaced by GIVA'A-TI's trademark bright purple beret. After the briefest of inspections, the men will head out for home. For the tracker, the end of a successful patrol is marked by the mandatory cup of Turkish coffee laced with cardamom. Although families, wives, and children are important to the Bedouin, most trackers feel married to their units and their jobs. After a quick Bedouin feast with his fellow trackers, Halil will clean his weapon and catch some shut-eye. After all, tomorrow is yet another day along the fence.

Not all security details along the fence are as uneventful. When the spontaneous Palestinian uprising on the West Bank and Gaza Strip commenced in early December 1987, the various Palestinian terror organizations based in Lebanon were determined to assume at least some vestiges of control over the disturbances. They attempted to achieve their objectives by staging spectacular cross-border attacks from Lebanese and even Jordanian territory. Most attempts were met with firepower and terminated. Toward the end of April 1988, however, just as Israel began to

celebrate its fortieth birthday, the Palestinians aided by their Lebanese Shiite allies decided to raise the ante of violence.

At dawn on 26 April, three members of Nayif Hawatmeh's Democratic Front for the Liberation of Palestine (DFLP) cut their way across the security fence separating Israel and Lebanon near Mount Dov to commit a terrorist act in one of the nearby agricultural settlements. Theirs was nicknamed "The Abu-Jihad Commando Force," a direct reference to martyred chief of PLO terrorist activities Abu-Jihad, killed in Tunis in a brilliant Israeli operation. The terrorists were heavily armed with AKMS 7.62mm assault ri-

Heavily ladened GIVA'ATI platoon commander informs HQ of a "mission accomplished" in Lebanon before boarding the CH-53 for the quick hop back to Israel.

fles, Russian F-1 antipersonnel grenades, and American LAW 66mm rockets. The moment the terrorists touched the fence, alarms were signaled, flares were fired, and a GIVA'ATI battalion was dispatched for the pursuit and kill.

Visibility was poor, with the spring sun at low profile and a blinding haze, and battalion commander Lt. Col. Shmuel Adiv realized the pursuit called for his personal attention. Just two weeks prior, he had commanded a successful pursuit of Palestinian terrorists aiming for Kfar Yuval. He summoned the battalion's chief tracker, Sgt. Ramzi Wachsh, and formed a spearhead to locate the infiltrators before they could reach a civilian target. Wachsh carefully followed the telltale footprints onto the mountain, leading Adiv and his squad of young and anxious conscripts into the underbrush. Suddenly a burst of automatic weapon fire erupted. In typical IDF fashion, Adiv sprinted forward and shouted "follow me!" They would be his last words. From two meters out, two terrorists fired 7.62mm bursts and a LAW rocket at the twenty-eight-year-old battalion commander, killing him instantly. Wachsh was in the process of warning his commander of the terrorist's positions when the firefight broke out, and he exposed his position in order to allow the others to take cover. He managed to fire his M-16, killing one of the terrorists, before a burst of AKMS fire ended his life. Thirty seconds later, the three-man terror squad was eliminated.

The following day, Lieutenant Colonel Adiv and Sergeant Wachsh were buried in highly emotional funerals. Adiv was survived by a wife and two children, and was remembered as a brilliant and courageous commander who would do anything and everything for his men. He had just received the rank of Lieutenant Colonel in a proud ceremony on Israel's fortieth birthday, and was hoping for a long career in the IDF. He had often wryly mentioned that if he had to die, he wanted to go leading his men, and indeed his morbid wish was fulfilled. Twenty-five-year-old Sergeant Wachsh was the eighth son of ten brothers, all trackers. He lived in the northern cooperative of Ya'ara, where Jewish and Bedouin families live side by side. His tragic death makes clear the

"HIT THE GROUND, BREATHE SLOWLY, TAKE AIM, AND FIRE!" A GIVA'ATI rifle grenadier practices what he'll probably be doing for real in the near future.

Some south Lebanese "toys" captured from a PLO arms cache during a preemptive Israeli raid.

Bedouins' contribution to Israel's defense: He was the fifth Wachsh brother, all trackers, to die in the line of duty.

Less than twenty-four hours after the firefight, Lieutenant Colonel Adiv's unit found itself in position to avenge the deaths of two of their own. The men had just returned from the emotional funerals, and hadn't even had time to remove their Class A uniforms when the alarm of the second infiltration attempt in as many days was sounded. The men quickly grabbed their gear and headed out to Mount Dov. These two terrorists belonged to a different PLO faction, the Palestinian Liberation Front (PLF) commanded by Abu al-Abbas, which was responsible for the seajacking of the *Achille Lauro* in 1985 and the murder of wheelchair-bound American Leon Klinghoffer. Their fate was the same as that of their DFLP comrades a day earlier. After firing at a civilian truck near the border, the terrorist duo headed into the thick Galilee wilderness. Led by the trackers and Lieutenant Colonel

Adiv's deputy battalion commander, Major A., a ninety-minute pursuit was conducted with the assistance of helicopter gunships. When contact was made, the firefight was brief and deadly. Captured documents disclosed that the infiltrators' intention was to seize and kill hostages at a nearby settlement. Their mission's termination was of some solace to the deputy battalion commander, who sadly commented: "We go on even though we've paid a dear price."

The high human cost of service in and around the Lebanese frontier is a remarkable motivating factor in the close-knit GIVA'ATI family. The day following the funeral of Lieutenant Colonel Adiv, a score of new GIVA'ATI conscripts were sworn into the IDF in an impressive ceremony held at the Wailing Wall in Jerusalem. Amid the family members, friends, and top brass, hundreds of GIVA'ATI trainees left the spartan conditions of IDF infantry training to take their vow of allegiance to Israel, the IDF, and the brigade.

The ceremony's commencement speaker was Colonel A., the GIVA'ATI Brigade commander. The thirty-six-year-old kibbutz-born colonel holds an extraordinary wealth of combat experience for his eighteen years of military duty, and is superbly qualified to lead the "purple brigade." He began his service with the naval commandos, but following a diving accident, transferred into the GOLANI Brigade. Following squad leaders and officer courses, he fought on the Golan Heights against the Syrian onslaught in 1973, where he was decorated for valor. He was then given command of SAYERET GOLANI, the brigade's elite reconnaissance force, and commanded one of the GOLANI forces that participated in the July 4th, 1976, rescue raid on Entebbe. Following Entebbe, Colonel A. was offered the command of another IDF elite unit, but declined, instead opting to embrace Orthodox Judaism. Today, his heavy beard and purple skullcap make him unique among infantry brigade commanders. Yet his warm demeanor and extraordinary exploits make him a figurehead, and the three hundred conscripts standing at attention in the cool Jerusalem eve embrace his words with enthusiasm and respect.

The topic of Colonel A.'s speech that night was, not surprisingly, the April 26th firefight atop Mount Dov, with an impassioned explanation of the soldiers' sacrifice and responsibility in safeguarding the state. Afterwards the young soldiers lined up to receive an army-issue bible, and swear on the holy scriptures and on their GALILs to faithfully defend the state of Israel. The procession's military precision was followed by a party atmosphere, where parents hugged and kissed their sons. The joyous atmosphere was controlled, however, by vigilance and tight security. Still fresh on everyone's mind was an incident that took place during a GIVA'ATI swearing-in ceremony in October 1986: Palestinian terrorists threw a Russian antipersonnel grenade at the gathering, killing one parent and wounding more than thirty soldiers.

The impressive swearing-in ceremony in Jerusalem anoints the soldiers into the brigade, but they will face many more obstacles before they can be considered true GIVA'ATI fighters. During the remaining months of infantry basic, the soldiers will undergo dehumanizing abuse at the hands of squad sergeants and officers, sleep but a few hours a night, and become deadly proficient in the use of tools of war, including GALIL and M-16 5.56mm assault rifles, the ubiquitous FN MAG 7.62mm light machine gun, the U.S.–made 66 LAWs, and the Soviet RPG-7, captured in such numbers from the Arabs that it is now an issue item.

Like all IDF combat units, the GIVA'ATI Brigade offers certain perks, mainly prized unit insignias, which represent unit pride, as well as individual pride. The soldiers must endure long and difficult forced marches to receive their brigade tunic pin and unit tags. The purple beret is given out last and is the hardest of all items to obtain: The price is an 80-kilometer forced march through some of Israel's most inhospitable terrain. All elite units have their infamous forced marches, and the 80-kilometer effort, in full combat gear and at a brutal pace, is one of the toughest. Those GIVA'ATI infantrymen who believe they are of a special breed are allowed to volunteer for the brigade's paratroop trained reconnaissance force, SAY-

GIVA'ATI infantrymen return to their Bell-212 following a search and destroy mission near the Lebanese border.

ERET GIVA'ATI. Terms of acceptance are a bit harsher, and include a 120-kilometer forced march usually completed in a mere twenty-six hours. Having passed the test, the proud young infantrymen assemble, and the SAYERET commander hands out berets until the rows of men become a sea of purple.

Once basic training is completed, the real duty begins. The men will be attached to various battalions; those showing the best leadership qualities will be chosen for squad leaders, and for the officers' course. They will spread throughout Israel, and, of course, Lebanon.

Back along the fence, another GIVA'ATI patrol sits tensely in their BATA'SHIT, when a tractor from one of the nearby settlements comes rolling by. As the soldiers greet the farmer, his young son waves and shouts a warm thank-you to the teenage soldiers, who remove one hand from their GALILs just long enough to wave in return. The reason for their vigil becomes tangibly clear, and the patrol continues.

Chapter 4
From Basic to Battle: "After the Paratroops!"

By all outward appearances, the paratroopers (TZANHANIM as they are known in Hebrew) are Israel's most striking soldiers. With red berets, shining silver jump wings, and brown leather paratroop boots, the paratroopers evoke a sense of power, and present a visual definition of the word "elite." Nowhere is this sense more imposing than on BA'K'UM, the IDF's version of Ellis Island. BA'K'UM is the Hebrew acronym for "Absorption and Assortment Base," a recruit depot where eighteen-year-old Israeli boys and girls fresh out of high school exchange Levis for fatigues, schoolbags for kit bags. BA'K'UM offers the newly conscripted soldiers the opportunity to decide their fate and destiny in the IDF, since almost any unit and profession are open. As always, the longest line for volunteers can be found underneath a huge khaki canvas tent, marked by a giant red sign in the shape of parachutist wings, with the emblazed logo ACHAREI HATZANHANIM: "After the Paratroops!"

The eighteen-year-old volunteers fidgeting in their newly issued olive fatigues have all dreamed of one day becoming paratroopers, for all the right and wrong reasons. There are those from the kibbutzim, reared

A paratrooper completes the first of the seven jumps which will qualify him for the coveted silver parachutist wings.

in an elitist psyche, who feel that volunteering for an elite commando unit is a guarantee against being outcast. Then there are those whose fathers, uncles, brothers, and sometimes even mothers have served in the paratroops; they see themselves as a natural

With his winter parka and mustache to keep him warm, a paratroop senior master sergeant offers a rare smile.

continuation of the family tradition. Sometimes their brothers or fathers have been killed in battle, and the soldier must present a hard-fought-for note from mother permitting them to volunteer. Many volunteer, however, simply for the chance to be the best. They are usually the most outstanding recruits of all. To them, successful service in the paratroops is a litmus test of their self-worth. They have been looking for this test of identity since adolescence, and vow not to back down. Whatever the reasons, these Israeli teenagers have been literally reared on the paratroop's battlefield exploits, and come to the army with the determination and humility to be pushed beyond their limits, and to one day wear the red beret.

Becoming a paratrooper isn't easy, and the nineteen-year-old sergeant assigned to introduce the young people to life in the paratroops is blunt, harsh, and painfully honest. He first allows the soldiers to look him over, letting everyone observe the way he wears his paratroop Class A uniform, his rank, his wings. The battle of impressions continues with a full tour

---

"EACH SOLDIER LINE UP. ASSUME THE POSITION. CHECK MAGAZINE. LOCK AND LOAD. EACH SOLDIER TO HIS *OWN* TARGET. AIM FOR IT . . . FIRE!!!!!" Paratroopers with their GALILS.

around the paratroop tent, in which GALILs, RPGs, LAWs, and even a jeep fitted with a TOW (tube-launched, optically tracked, wire-guided) missile are on display. The sight of weaponry and equipment creates quick illusions of grandeur; soon every paratroop hopeful envisions himself leading a mission-impossible commando raid against some impregnable fortress in Beirut or Damascus. The image is immediately shattered when the more sobering part of the introduction begins. The assembled hopefuls are offered a glimpse at the sergeant's Lebanon scars, followed by a somber reading of the tally of paratroopers killed in Lebanon, and those horribly wounded. Many of the casualties, the sergeant adds, were his close friends. With the silence in the tent so thick it can be cut, a checklist of paratroop requirements is shouted aloud: Five months of grueling infantry basic training, one month of jump school, and operational duty in the ''mud, sand, and the misery until you are too old to even be a reservist!'' Having disillusioned as many of the soldiers as possible, the sergeant then goes into a highly impassioned speech as to why the paratroops are such a trenchant element in Israel's fight for survival. It is clearly a lesson of life and death — remarkable considering the instructor is but a year older than his pupils.

Lining up to volunteer does not secure the soldier his chance to earn the red beret. There are numerous stumbling blocks placed in front of the dream, the first being a four-hour minitest period called a GIBUSH. The GIBUSH allows the commander to distinguish between soldiers who look good on paper and those who will perform up to standard in the field. All hopefuls are issued numbers and are ushered onto a small, parched field, where they will push their untapped leg muscles through laps, negotiate obstacles, and perform difficult physical exercises for an inspecting team of NCOs. Through each young soldier's performance, the NCO is able to determine not only the candidate's physical limits, but most importantly his character. A soldier who completes the course

After learning how to march and shoot, paratroop hopefuls check their weapons before beginning a desert patrol.

with ease yet gives little encouragement to his comrades is looked down upon, whereas a soldier who barely makes it yet gives his all receives high marks and an eventual thumbs-up. It is the classic military virtues of reliability and comradeship that are sought, and best predicted by the GIBUSH.

Following the mandatory psychological interview before a board of paratroop officers, the soldiers will soon learn their fate for the next three years. Realizing that paratroop basic is often brutal, the officers in charge of the GIBUSH must weed out those they think won't mentally and physically survive TIRONUT (basic training). While the officers make their choices, the men wait outside the fabricated concrete hut decorated with pictures of smiling soldiers extolling the virtues of wearing your uniform with pride. Many of the young soldiers have already finished their second pack of Time cigarettes in anxious anticipation; some joke about their remaining days in the military —

"3 down, only 1,092 to go!" Others sit in silence.

A captain finally emerges from the deliberation with the GIBUSH results. A quick "attention" order gets the rabble in line, and the names are read aloud. Those accepted explode in cries of relief, then assemble themselves in a tough "paratroop-like" pose beside their heavy kit bags. The unfortunate majority are placed in line and sent back to "mainstream BA-'K'UM," where they will continue their search for a suitable job in the IDF. Most seem depressed: Their hopes for the red beret have been dashed and they realize they will probably be sent to the Armored Corps to live amid the noise, dust, mud, and claustrophobia of tanks. Others will become artillery crewmen, mechanized infantrymen, or desk-bound "jobniks." Most depressing is the return to BA'K'UM, to its cleaning of latrines and pots.

The next obstacle along the route to becoming a paratrooper is the most difficult — basic training. The training camp is only a ninety-minute ride from BA-'K'UM, located on the West Bank, yet the short journey seems like an eternity. The talk aboard the bus is marked by the brave telling the fainthearted about "how easy basic will be"! Such bravado sparks the thirty-eight-year-old reservist driver and the accompanying officer, and they start to chuckle, which in turn produces a humiliating silence.

When the bus reaches its destination, the feelings of helplessness are only magnified. Standing on the muddy grounds, amid rows of mud-stained tents and mud-covered concrete cubes masquerading for buildings, is the welcoming committee — three smartly dressed sergeants and an officer with menacing eyes armed with a clipboard. The relaxed atmosphere of BA'K'UM is replaced by shouts and orders. Immediately, the men are ordered to fall in line, in rows of

three, "in thirty seconds . . . now!" As other buses from BA'K'UM arrive, the motley assembly is divided into companies, platoons, and squads, identifiable only by small, colored pieces of tape, substituting for rank, worn across epaulets. The squads are then ushered to their tents, and for the first time the realization dawns that they will be sleeping outside in the chilly Judean Hill nights. The grumbling and complaints are terminated by the squad sergeant's shouts for silence and the order to line up outside "in thirty seconds . . . MOVE!" Welcome to the paratroops!

The first introduction the men enjoy is that of their squad leader, a cynical first sergeant named Roni, who will lead ALEPH or "A" Squad. What is perhaps so interesting about the methods of IDF combat unit training is that all of the squad leaders, Roni included, are conscripts completing their three years of national service. The IDF does not maintain a rank or function of drill instructor. Instead, most squad leaders are

Paratroop candidates march to their physical limits. The reward will be the coveted paratroop trademark: the red beret!

Another paratroop trademark, and source of enormous pride: the winged snake symbol is the paratroop brigade's infamous calling card.

NCOs being punished for not accepting the invitation to "BAHAD 1," the IDF's Officer School. Most of them have but a few months left in their three years of active service, and the brigade commander hopes that one taste of command will make them see the light. In most cases, the pressure tactic doesn't work, although the resentment it produces does turn an "old-timer" counting out his remaining days into a commander with just the right amount of bitterness, discipline, and compassion. Many of the squad leaders abhor the fact that their men look upon them as heartless monsters, but find no other choice. Roni, who has spent more than his share of nights in Lebanon, is quick to point out: "Being a paratrooper is serious and deadly business. I'd much rather command a soldier who hates me and survives, than one who loves me and ends up dead!"

Next, the three squads of 3d Platoon meet their commander, a twenty-two-year-old first lieutenant named Uzi. Like the weapon whose name he bears, Lieutenant Uzi is a compact compilation of efficiency, reliability, and killing power. His cool blue eyes are the window to his past, and each soldier staring at him can see months of harsh duty on the West Bank, in Lebanon, and perhaps points beyond. They can also see that he is not to be crossed. Speaking with the confidence of one much higher in rank and years, Uzi marches up and down the ranks, delivering a painful lesson in paratroop folklore. One by one Uzi lists landmark achievements in IDF paratroop history: the first battalion formed in 1949, the Mitla Pass in 1956, the liberation of Jerusalem in 1967, the Jordan Valley in 1969, the "Chinese Farm" in 1973, Entebbe in 1976, and finally Beirut in 1982. He says that "following the paratroops is following a map of the Middle East." He concludes by telling the now-exhausted men the importance of the 1,265 paratroopers killed in the past forty years and seven wars, and his determination to make life such hell for them in training that *they* won't become statistics.

Lieutenant Uzi is typical of the commissioned paratroop officer, truly the best of the IDF. Having spent more than two years in the brigade as NCOs, and then more than a year as commissioned officers, the platoon commanders bring their conscripts a wide range of practical and textbook experience. They have been selected specifically to be instructors, and have been taught unique command skills that allow them to draw upon actual personal battlefield experience. Consequently, most textbook guidelines are discarded in favor of the skills born of life-and-death decisions that they have observed their own commanders make in the heat of battle. These officers also possess the special talent of recognizing leadership qualities similar to their own, and will make note of conscripts who display these characteristics.

What will be absent from the following six months of indoctrination is the intimidation so noticeable in other armies. Inside this base atop a stoic ridge, there is no sadistic though well-intentioned drill instructor (DI) to rally the men with cadence calls in a premorning run. Even though such a system of training has worked for the U.S. Marine Corps for more than 200 years, it would never work in Israel, a small country whose citizens have very defined Middle Eastern egos and pride. It is also unnecessary. The eighteen-year-old conscripts who have volunteered for the TZANHANIM do not need the tirades of a "crew cut wearing stripes" to push them. With Palestinian and Shiite terrorists in Lebanon, Syrian T-72s on the Golan, and the highly professional Jordanian Army nearby, all the motivation these men need is right across the borders.

As Lieutenant Uzi finishes his address and exits the hall, the men stand up in an impromptu salute, and then follow their sergeants to the tents, hopefully for some sleep. Already, everything is done on a quick run. The conscripts haven't walked since BA-'K'UM and won't walk again until they're out of the army. The running is meant to keep the body and mind always moving, and the new soldiers realize that they had better get used to it.

After marching 15 kilometers under a brutal desert sun, a paratrooper FN MAG light machine-gunner catches one last breath before filling his target full of neat 7.62mm holes.

Future paratroopers being taught the "how to's" of built-up area combat. The bullet holes attest to the generations of fighters to have passed through these corridors.

Before ALEPH squad can rest their tired heads on the Israeli soldier's version of a pillow — a rolled-up issue olive winter parka — Sergeant Roni will pick a HANICH TORAN, or "cadet commander." The cadet commander is an integral element of IDF training. While he holds no direct command or authority, he is the squad's ambassador to the outside chain of command. His main function is insuring that all orders are carried out in the prescribed time allotted. When the squad sergeant shouts "you have thirty seconds to be assembled in front," it will be the cadet commander who will shout, carry on, and, if necessary, use force to help the squad meet its deadline. The NCOs and officers will judge each soldier's leadership capabilities by observing the HANICH TORAN in action. The soldier also realizes the importance of the HANICH TORAN, since his chances for squad leader and officers' courses all depend on his performance as cadet commander. ALEPH squad's first HANICH TORAN is Private Shmulik, and almost twenty hours after their bus leaves BA'K'UM, Private Shmulik is authorized to order his men to sleep. It's been a long first day.

Nobody will sleep that first night. Under a brilliant starlit sky, the eighteen men of ALEPH squad will begin to bond into a cohesive identity. The men are as diverse as they are united, but all seek a helping hand and shoulder to lean on. Some cope with the first night as if it were nothing, especially Ilan, an eighteen-year-old graduate of Israel's only military academy. The academy mainly accepts children from broken homes. Being raised by a single parent never seemed a handicap for Ilan. With four years of education and military discipline behind him, Ilan finds himself in a perfect position to meet the challenges of the paratroops. He is already considered a corporal by the IDF (although he won't wear his ranks on base), and has made seven jumps (although the scorn of his NCOs forbids him from placing the wings on his Class A tunic). He is a leader among the squad, and when the first inspection arrives, like the first of everything else, ALEPH squad will turn to Ilan.

In the paratroops, like the rest of the IDF, little importance is given to spit and polish, or the pomp and ceremony characteristic of so many Western ar-

mies. A paratrooper or GOLANI infantryman might march 100 kilometers to earn the honor of wearing the brigade's distinctive beret, but the same person will offer striking resistance to ironing his trousers or shining his boots. Accepting the Israeli mentality for what it is, and recognizing the fact that the real reason for conscripting an army is for defense, not parade, IDF basic training concentrates on the art of weapons proficiency.

Before the eighteen-year-old conscript can become a deadly tool, however, he must be broken and re-molded in order to be taught the discipline of combat. TIRONUT achieves this objective through intensive

The paratrooper's workhorse, the C-130 Hercules, kicks up a cloud of covering dust during a training assault.

physical examinations, menial labor around the base, and pointless duties. Without physically or mentally abusing the conscript, the NCOs and officers try to make the soldier realize that he is part of a large machine, and that he is expected to function all the time, and on demand! Although the IDF promotes, even welcomes, innovation, these new men must be taught to serve the IDF before they can begin shaping its course.

Everything in the lives of the conscripts for the next six months will be done within the framework of the squad or KITA. Squads will sleep, eat, learn, fire, march, and sweat together. It is much simpler to break the newly conscripted soldiers in their lowest possible denominator, and the squad soon becomes that identifiable entity. Yet before the squad can advance to real military training, let alone exercises at the platoon level, it will have to learn the basics of soldiering, especially wake-up at 0500! Soon the reality and routine of life in the paratroops become all too apparent: Wake-up, morning inspection, food not fit to eat, physical training, pointless menial labor,

discomfort, more physical training, homesickness, instruction, discipline indoctrination, nonexistent free time, evening inspection, and of course much more physical training before lights out.

Day two of basic means a GALIL. After much anticipation, ALEPH squad runs through the thick, rust-colored mud toward the armory shack. After Lieutenant Uzi makes a brief speech on the meaning of the weapon, as well as the mandatory "this is not a toy,

Another workhorse in paratrooper service, the CH-53 helicopter, seen here ferrying a platoon of battle-equipped paratroopers to an anonymous spot near the Lebanese border.

49

et cetera,'' a forty-year-old reservist hands each soldier a 5.56mm Israel Military Industries GALIL assault rifle. At first, the soldiers don't know what to do with the weapons. They hold them in firing poses that would make John Wayne blush, and make tommy-gun noises; a quick shout from Sergeant Roni brings them back to reality. For his squad's inability to wait for ''action,'' Roni promises them guard duty around the base perimeter, even though it will be some time before magazines and ammunition are issued. Slowly but surely, however, the soldiers of ALEPH squad are beginning to look like fighters.

ALEPH squad is allowed to hold the sacred weapons just long enough for each man to memorize his GALIL's serial number, then the guns are returned to the reservist armorer. The men won't be formally attached to their weapons until the swearing-in ceremonies, when they take the solemn oath to army, country, and God. In the meantime, ALEPH squad will continue to pitch tents, clean out latrines, and be subjected to push-ups, sit-ups, and other means of physical torture.

Three days later, ALEPH squad finds itself on the road to Jerusalem, toward the Wailing Wall and an emotional gathering. During the 1967 Six Day War, the 55th Reserve Paratroop Brigade captured the Old City of Jerusalem from a well-entrenched Jordanian force. The battles were fierce; at Ammunition Hill it was hand-to-hand combat for five savage hours. The paratroopers persevered, however, and by the second day of the war, Temple Mount, the site of Judaism's two destroyed temples, was in the hands of the red berets. All that remains in testament is the wall, a single tangible relic of Jewish survival. The Jordanians had forbidden Jewish worship at the wall, and its return to Israel signaled pious celebration the world over, as well as an eternal debt to the paratroops. As a result, all paratroop and most elite-unit swearing-in ceremonies are held before this backdrop of past and present, holy and mighty.

The ceremony is quick and to the point. While parents, girlfriends, and the curious assemble behind security barriers, a battalion of men in khaki-green berets marches in crude though passable formation to the predesignated positions. Alongside each platoon, three officers stand beside a table loaded with navy blue paperback bibles and a stack of GALILS in a blue wooden carrier, arranged to give each soldier the same weapon he signed for days earlier. For this particular ceremony, Chief of Staff Lt. Gen. Dan Shomron, the hero of Entebbe and himself a former paratroop commander, will be in attendance, a fact heavy on the minds of *all* soldiers present. When the Chief of Staff's procession makes its way toward the podium, the recruits can't help but turn their heads and sneak a peek; it takes the shouts of all the squad sergeants to bring everyone back into line.

After brief speeches by the Chief of Staff and the paratroop brigade commander, the platoon commanders order their men to the table one by one, where they are brusquely handed their GALIL and a bible. Each man gives the officer a rare though wholehearted IDF salute. The ceremony concludes with the oath. As the lights around the Wailing Wall are dimmed and a huge wooden mock-up of paratroop wings is lit, the men recite the following:
I hereby swear, and fully commit myself, to be faithful to the State of Israel, to its constitution and its authorities, and to take it upon myself, without reservations or hesitancy, the rules of discipline of the Israel Defense Forces, to obey all commands and orders given by authorized commanders, and to devote all my strengths, and even sacrifice my life, to the defense of my country and the freedom of Israel.
The oath signals the end of ''playtime,'' and following the quick ride back to base, hell will soon begin.

At 0330 the following morning, ALEPH squad is awakened to an ''American inspection.'' In three minutes, they are ordered to move all their personal belongings to the central flagpole, fifty meters from their tents. The morning sun has yet to rise and frigid winds are whistling as eighteen men appear, laden

with personal gear, kit bags, and army cots. New
cadet commander Ilan frantically tries to rally the
squad together, but it is a pitiful exercise in futility.
The squad is late by ninety-five seconds. It will be
put on account when weekend passes are issued, and
Lieutenant Uzi makes a notation of it in his despised
little red notebook. After a quick inspection, almost
too quick for the misery it has caused, ALEPH squad
returns to its tent, and the remaining thirty minutes
of sleep. They'll need it! Lieutenant Uzi has promised
a ten-kilometer forced march for good measure.

The forced march, with its jerrycans, AN/PRC-

As training progresses, the paratroopers begin to patrol in
fully operational surroundings, here a seaside stretch of
border with Lebanon near Rosh Hanikra.

25 radios, and stretcher bearers, is a conditioning
exercise with very definite objectives. Not only does
the harsh physical reality of the march produce inner
strength, but there are more practical benefits: When
one day the soldier finds himself cut off behind enemy
lines, knowing how to delegate body strength for a
twenty-kilometer march might be the deciding factor
in saving his life. Soon, however, twenty kilometers

Welcome to Maidun! As paratroopers purify the town of its well-armed *Hizballah* inhabitants, the covering armor force stands in the approaching roads awaiting any call for help.

will seem like a stroll through the countryside, and there are still hundreds of klicks to be negotiated on foot.

As the men assemble with full gear, they are placed in a double line, and the race into the unknown begins. At first the pace is quick though manageable, and only the arm muscles, unaccustomed to carrying weapons without slings, are protesting. A few moments later, the stretcher is ordered open, and the squad's largest individual, Moshe, a 100-kilo-plus hulk from Soviet Georgia, is ordered to play the wounded soldier. It's the first lesson in the importance of caring

for the wounded. Sergeant Roni is quick to threaten that, should Moshe be dropped, he will be carried for the next six months! The stretcher is hoisted above four unfortunate shoulders, and the pace intensifies to a brutal scurry. When one of the stretcher-bearers feels he can no longer maintain the burden, a hand is raised and another soldier takes over. The stretcher march is a carefully orchestrated exercise in building unit cohesion and reliability, which it is hoped will be embedded in the mind of each soldier.

A soldier who fails to answer his comrade's plea for assistance is labeled by the squad as SOTZIOMAT or "selfish one." This is the soldier who never shares gift parcels or gives a helping hand during trying physical ventures. Although, in training, such soldiers might enjoy more food or rest, in the field the reputation of SOTZIOMAT is a lonely and irreversible one. During a cross-border patrol or firefight, every squad member knows which soldier is not to be relied upon; this person also will receive little sympathy or effort in the event of injury. Sergeant Roni realizes that the "SOTZIOMAT syndrome" is best nipped in the bud, and as a result he orders Private Gilad, ALEPH squad's selfish one, "front and center." He is given the thirty-kilogram-plus jerrycan of water and is ordered to march right next to the NCO until he drops. To reinforce this lesson, Sergeant Roni intensifies the march's pace, until it is impossible for the squad to catch up. Ten kilometers and a few hours later, the brutal rite of passage will end, and ALEPH squad will enjoy

---

"Before you can earn your wings, you must learn how to fly!" A young paratroop hopeful leaps from the "Eichmann," Tel Nof's infamous jump tower.

a robust morale builder to last them through the endless line of forced marches to follow.

Following the early morning march, the squad heads toward the weapons tent, where basic instruction on the GALIL will commence. Within the next few days, the squad will learn the GALIL's basic anatomy, and will be able to recite the stripping process: Remove *receiver;* pull out *return spring;* extend *charging handle;* and remove *bolt, bolt carrier,* and finally *gas cylinder.* They'll also conduct this exercise in a muddy field at night so that in a matter of days, they'll have mastered the process well enough to do it blindfolded

After six months of brutal basic training, only one obstacle remains before the soldiers can truly be called TZANHANIM: the Tel Nof parachuting school.

in less than ten seconds. They'll learn to fire the weapon in a multitude of poses, and learn to destroy a fortified position with a rifle grenade. This routine of constant forced marches and weapons training will be ALEPH squad's way of life for the next three months.

A striking aspect of paratroop training is the number of weapons on which each soldier is trained. Forty years ago, the budding IDF had to make do with a few stolen and homemade Sten submachine guns and a small supply of Czech K98 Mausers. Today, few armies can boast the variety and quality of weaponry supplied to the Israeli soldier, and the commanders make sure their men know all their deadly secrets. They'll learn to squeeze off shots with the obsolete though still potent UZI submachine gun; fire the M-16 family; provide cover fire with the 7.62mm FN MAG; snipe at long range with the M-21, Israel's updated version of the M-14; and for good measure, learn what makes the AK-47 Kalachnikov such a world-renowned weapon. Since every Israeli infantryman enjoys a dual, sometimes even triple, support weapons role within the squad, every soldier also learns why the infantryman is the tank's greatest nemesis, especially when equipped with the likes of the LAW, the RPG-7, and the Dragon. The men are taught how to lob a few 52mm mortar shells with deadly accuracy, as well as toss an Mk. 26 antipersonnel grenade with the finesse of a center fielder (even though nobody plays baseball in Israel!). To compensate for all the instruction in destruction, each re-

The training is over, and the nervous paratroopers await their first real jump.

A majestic sight if ever there was one: paratroopers fall from the sky, out of the belly of a C-130 Hercules.

cruit also receives more than sixty hours of medical training.

Three months into the training, the once motley-looking group of paratroop cadets now appears to be a formidable fighting machine. There is still plenty of work to be done before the trainees can be qualified as "riflemen 5th class," and the training continues at a brutal pace. Once the squad knows what to do with its weapons, intersquad, interplatoon, and inter-company exercises commence. Learning tactics and strategy in the classroom is quite different from as-saulting a fortified bunker in the winter mud, lugging fifty kilos on your back. Behind the assaulting squad is the sergeant, who takes great care to violently slap the helmets of soldiers not falling into firing position in the instructed manner. "You're dead, you're dead, you're dead, and you're horribly wounded," shouts Sergeant Roni, whose hands already ache from bash-ing his men's helmets. The defending squad members are also hit by their sergeant for failing to pour fire into the oncoming masses. Intimidation breeds innova-tion, and the slaps stop only when the soldiers show some improvement.

Soon, maneuvers begin, and maneuvers mean APCs (armored personnel carriers). After years of disdaining mechanization, almost every Israeli combat unit now relies on the American-made M113 for trans-port under fire. During the 1973 War, the M113 fleets ferried GOLANI infantrymen toward Damascus and paratroopers toward Cairo. Although they were instru-mental in the eventual Israeli victory, the M113s were devastated by Arab Saggers (anti-tank missiles) and RPGs. The M113 fleets were refitted with add-on armor plating, and in Lebanon, they brought Israeli forces into battle against a well-entrenched Palestinian defender, all the way to Beirut and back. They became the infantry's mobile home and, with a complement of 52mm mortar, FN MAGs, and .50-caliber machine guns, a hefty fire-support base.

Just as important as the M113 is the helicopter, the paratroops' quickest form of airborne deployment.

After a month of training in the art of rappeling on a mountain named MIFLETZET or "monster," it's time for the helos. The impressive arrival of five Bell-212s painted in mud brown brings about excitement and fear. Soon the Bell-212s are airborne, flying high atop the biblical landscape, marked only by an army ambulance racing in pursuit on the ground below. One by one the men are ordered down the thick coils of rope suspended from the helos. Fear and hesitation are outranked by shouts from an impatient paratroop captain, and soon a majority of the men are down the ropes to the hard earth below, and congratulations for a job well done.

The final month of paratroop basic is filled with numerous educational excursions throughout the na-tion. From the snowy peaks of Mount Hermon to the desert wilderness near the Egyptian frontier, the soldiers will see and learn more about their nation and heritage than four years of high school could ever have hoped to accomplish. The IDF, besides its role in defending the state, is also Israel's largest

"JUMP! GET YOUR ASS OUT OF HERE NOW!" First timers sometimes need the instructor's foot in the backside.

educational facility, and the soldier is of little use if he doesn't know why and for what he'll be fighting. The teachers for the week-long trip are a group of female soldiers whose intelligence and enormous good looks gain everyone's attention. Minds do not wander for long, however, as one formidable obstacle remains — the MASA'A MESAKEM, or hundred-kilometer "commencement march." Already fear has given way to reason: After all, the soldiers did survive the sixty-kilometer "unit tag" run and the brutal eighty-kilometer red beret haul. The soldiers can be heard mumbling to themselves a familiar war cry: "If I don't pass this, I'm not a man!"

The march will begin at home base and wind its way along the West Bank through the rocky Judean Hills toward Jerusalem. The April heat has emerged, so the hundred klicks will prove three times as hard as the red beret march. For a week the soldiers have been training and conditioning their bodies and minds for the torturous twenty-plus hour event. At 1500 on a bright and beautiful April day, the entire battalion lines up for inspection before the base commander. They wear full battle gear, carry their personal and squad support weapons, and are ablaze with confidence — a striking contrast to what walked into base half a year earlier.

The march sets out at a feverish pace, led by the base commander, and followed by what is hoped will be the paratroop brigade's next graduating class. For the next twenty hours, the soon-to-be riflemen 5th class will cross much of the Israeli landscape. Every kilometer will be paid for in sweat, aching muscles, and the achievement of a goal of which few can boast. The marching procession enters Jerusalem along the same route the 55th Brigade took when it liberated the city from the tenacious Jordanians. The remaining few kilometers through Jerusalem are completed in a brisk run. The panting mass of olive and khaki passes Ammunition Hill and Shiekh Jarakh, and for the second time in five months, the soldiers arrive at the Temple Mount, the Wailing Wall, and the end of a long haul.

The final obstacle remaining in training is Tel Nof air base, parachuting school, and most importantly, the jump instructor. Compared to basic training, Tel Nof is considered a TCHUPAR, or "gift given only to soldiers." There are no more forced marches, no 0500 wake-ups, and no more of the indignations of being a recruit. For the next thirty-odd days, the basic training graduates will learn the art of parachuting — even though the last IDF combat jump was in 1956 and the advent of helicopters has made most parachute assaults obsolete. The jumps, however, are what distinguish the paratrooper from his GIVA'ATI and GOLANI comrades. It's an exercise in military necessity, one deeply entrenched in tradition. All of Israel's most famous warriors have undergone the "Tel Nof Experience," and this new line of paratroopers look forward to it with anticipation and fear.

For those who fear the thought of jumping from an airplane, time has run out to back down, especially once the instructor arrives — a beautiful twenty-year-old sergeant named Sigal. There are only a few female jump instructors in the IDF, but the fact remains that male soldiers would rather die than act like cowards in front of a female instructor. This is especially important during the first jump, when first timers tend to dig their fingernails deep into the plane's fuselage before the instructor offers a smart kick in the backside for reassurance. That reality is still a few weeks down the road; Sigal has yet to introduce her class to the basics.

The training is intense and fast paced, although enjoyable. The roar of aircraft at Tel Nof makes being attentive in class difficult, but each paratrooper knows that mastering the Type EFA-672-12 (IS) main line and the T-10 reserve chute is what will keep him alive when the doors swing open and the green light flashes. The academics are meant to sharpen the jumper's mind, whereas the physical training increases his ability to withstand injuries, which are numerous. Before the jump itself, the paratroopers must experience the "Eichmann," the menacing jump tower that earned its nickname because of its resemblance to a gallows. Although it's not even forty feet high, the tower scares the bravest among the group, especially when the gear is hooked on, and the painful thrill of jump simulation is endured for the first time.

Three weeks of the Eichmann and countless hours later, Sigal escorts her silent class toward the tarmac, and the C-130 Hercules that will drop them. According to her, the pupils are as ready as they'll ever be. While boarding the sand-, green-, and mud-colored C-130 — the IAF's hero of Entebbe — Sigal is quick to point out that "it's a pity you guys won't be jumping from a C-47 so you can see how it was done by some real men back in 1956!" This is little consolation to the white-faced, jittery pupils. In forty minutes, a green light goes on, the exits take place at one-second intervals, and it's all over.

Six jumps later, including one at night, and the "bastards of November" are finally issued their silver metal jump wings, to be worn proudly above their hearts. The wings, red beret, and survival of basic training mean acceptance into a family of fighters including the likes of Arik Sharon, "Raful" Eitan, and Dan Shomron. Yet all the jump wings really guarantee is two and a half years of hard work, humping the earth with forty-kilo packs, and probable combat duty. Even though the soldiers learned how to parachute, the most useful skills they'll draw upon will be the survival taught in basic.

While the new paratroops were enjoying their one-week leave following jump school, their comrades were fighting for their lives in Lebanon — not in exhilarating para jumps but in hand-to-hand combat with a fanatical enemy. Palestinian terrorists there were being assisted by *Hizballah,* the fanatic Islamic Party of God responsible for the suicide car-bombing of the U.S. Embassy and Marine barracks in Beirut. *Hizballah* had converted the once-peaceful Shiite village of Maidun, which lay just fourteen kilometers from the Israeli frontier, into a major terrorist base, turning every roof into an AA position, every house into a bunker. About eighty terrorists guarded the village, and had vowed to martyr themselves rather

"Welcome to the paratroops!" A swearing-in ceremony at the Wailing Wall.

than submit to the "infidel" IDF. At 0530 on the hazy morning of 4 May, the paratroopers struck.

The lead paratroop vanguard of M113s found itself under immediate *Hizballah* fire the moment it entered the sleepy village. Supported by helicopter gunships, artillery, and tank fire, the paratroops dismounted their APCs and cleared the village the way they were trained to — on foot! They engaged the *Hizballah* terrorists in street-to-street, house-to-house, room-to-room fighting, which would last for twelve hours. The terrorists fought with fanatical determination, and dozens of battles raged. Most of the fighting was hand to hand, with such ferocity displayed that RPGs and LAWs were used as close-quarter weapons. When it was over, fifty *Hizballah* terrorists lay killed, and Maidun was wiped off the face of the map by more than 500 kilograms of high explosives. The paratroopers returned to Israel with sixteen wounded and the bodies of three of their own — company commander Capt. Tzion Mizrahi, Capt. Boaz Ravid, and Sgt. Marco Bernshtein. As always, the paratroops were called upon to deal with the most difficult military objectives, and, as always, the paratroops had accomplished their mission, no matter what the price. "After the Paratroops" indeed!

Chapter 5
Zealots in Black Berets: The Tank Soldiers' Story

Israel is a land of symbols, and METZADA is one of its most endearing. Situated in the middle of the barren Judean Desert and overlooking the misty shores of the mysterious Dead Sea, the cliff-top summer palace to King Herod owns a unique spot in Jewish history. In A.D. 73, nine hundred sixty Jewish zealots facing an overwhelming Roman force chose death over surrender, committing mass suicide rather than face the indignity of enslavement. METZADA's inspiring legacy of desperate courage is not lost to the IDF, which, like the nation it defends, is an army of symbols.

METZADA's message of last-stand heroics is one held very dear in the hearts and minds of Israel's tank soldiers. Their armored vehicles serve as the steel ring protecting the nation from being overrun. For the Armored Corps, holding your ground against an invader means victory; defeat would mean the second METZADA in 2,000 years. It is a brutal responsibility for an eighteen year old to bear. It is fitting, perhaps prophetic, that the Armored Corps chose the ruins at METZADA as the site where its recruits swear an oath of allegiance to the army and state. In this moving ceremony, with the soldier clutching his GALIL rifle and gazing at a wooden sign proclaiming "METZADA shall not fall again," he will for the first time realize why he is taking an oath amid a monument to death and self-sacrifice. After all, it's what service in HEYL SHIRION, the IDF Armored Corps, is all about.

Tanks lying in ambush, waiting for the order to advance.

An M-60 buries one of its targets on the first shot. A good tank crew will turn its target into a flaming hulk within three shots.

In this age of counterinsurgency warfare, "special forces," and commando operations, the importance of the tank soldier has been somewhat overlooked. Their contribution is just as important, if not more so, than that of the red-bereted paratrooper, the purple-bereted GIVA'ATI foot soldier, and the brown-bereted GOLANI rifleman. It takes just as much courage to engage the enemy from a tank as it does to leap from a helicopter behind enemy lines and attack a terrorist-held stronghold. Nevertheless, service in the Armored Corps is not voluntary. To be eligible for service with the Armored Corps, one doesn't need to run in record time, be in exemplary physical shape, or possess impressive intelligence. The only criteria an eighteen-year-old Israeli male heading into the army needs in order to one day wear the black beret and Armored Corps badge is average health and the knowledge that for the next three years of his life he'll have to "work his ass off" with three strangers in a sixty-ton vehicle. He'll have to fight off claustrophobia, live with mud and dust, and be a target for RPG projectiles heading toward him at a mere 300 meters per second!

There was a time when service in the Armored Corps was considered a fate worth than death. It was the chilling winter of 1973 and Israel had just survived one of its most traumatic wars. A tank war, where the wall of steel created by Centurion, Patton, and even obsolete Sherman tanks managed not only to save the nation, but push on toward Cairo and Damascus. It was a costly war as well. More than 2,500 Israeli soldiers had been killed in just eighteen days, and the great majority of them were tank soldiers. Fifteen years later, the Armored Corps has evolved into IDF's largest and also one of its most popular branches. According to Brig. Gen. Yossi Ben-Hanan, the highly decorated current Armored Corps commander who led a battalion of Centurions heading toward Damascus in 1973, HEYL SHIRION is in an "electrified state of morale." Of all the new tank soldiers conscripted in 1988, ninety-two percent of them had picked tanks as their first choice for service! With more than four wars of service in tanks behind him, Brigadier General Ben-Hanan has perhaps the greatest understanding of what it takes for the IDF Armored Corps to succeed, and he likes what he sees. Most importantly for Brigadier General Ben-Hanan, the majority of those volunteering into "tanks" are soldiers who didn't make the grade when volunteering for pilots' course, naval officers' course, and for the various paratroop reconnaissance units. Rejection for these men means one of two things — becoming a dreaded "jobnik" (an administrative soldier) or racing with kit bag in hand to the Armored Corps tent, where they beg for a spot on the next bus going to basic training. Welcome to the Armored Corps!

Basic training in the Armored Corps is identical to that for combat engineers, GOLANI and GIVA'ATI infantrymen, and the paratroops, except that it lasts for twelve weeks. It is a basic infantry routine meant to install a sense of combat proficiency into the heart and mind of each soldier. The lessons of the tank battles waged in Sinai in 1967, the Golan Heights in 1973, and Lebanon's Beka'a Valley in 1982 have taught the Armored Corps that the battle doesn't end once a tank has been hit by enemy fire. The critical key to victory in tank warfare is survival, and to survive, the "tankist" usually has to fight his way back to "friendly lines." As a result, the future MERKAVA gunners, Patton drivers, and Centurion loaders enjoy an intensive regiment of forced marches, infantry weapon firing, more forced marches, and individual combat training.

Private Kobi, an eighteen-year-old trainee from Haifa who has dreamed of riding in a MERKAVA for a good many years, has difficulty understanding why he must march fifty kilometers in the mud and rain with an AN/PRC-77 on his back when he'll be crouching inside a tank for the next three yeras. Kobi's look of exhausted confusion isn't lost on his platoon commander, twenty-year-old Lieutenant Yehuda, who barks at him: "That stupid look on your face won't

save your life when a Syrian commando hunts you down twenty klicks inside bandit country!'' The short, crisp speech is directed at the entire platoon, and brings the now self-reflecting rabble into a neat, fast-paced march.

Although the basic trainees will not learn a single aspect of armored warfare during their twelve weeks of infantry instruction, they will be taken on regular visits to active tank units throughout Israel, from a MERKAVA brigade station only yards away from Syrian lines on the Golan Heights to a force of M-60 Pattons stationed in the desert wasteland of the Jordan Valley. They will be introduced to the smells of diesel fuel

Caked with dust, soot, and the filth of living in the field, a reservist MERKAVA commander guides his vehicle across the firing range.

and smoking exhaust systems, and to soldiers, just like they will be in a few months, milling about covered with dust, grease, and mud. Yet perhaps the most poignant trip these recruits will take is to a tank base of another kind — a parking lot of destroyed and abandoned T-55s and T-62s retrieved from the Syrians during the 1982 Lebanon fighting. Platoon after platoon of basic trainees are sent to this base

The tank soldiers' nemesis, and greatest ally in all-out armor combat, the Hughes Defender-500 attack helicopter. With its TOW missiles, it is a formidable weapon.

somewhere in central Israel under the guise of performing cleanup duty; yet the real purpose of their visit is a crucial step in the education process of the Israeli tanker. As the men, who have been in uniform for only two months, slowly make their way across a parking lot with hundreds of destroyed and mangled vehicles in the Syrian camouflage scheme, they can for the first time see just how delicate 153mm of armor protection really can be. As the cleanup operation continues, the men notice a T-62 with its turret lying inverted over a charred chassis — a horrifying testament to the destructive capabilities of 1980s anti-

tank weapons. Standing near the twisted remnants of a once-mighty vehicle is a mountain of a master sergeant, who indicates the two points of impact caused by a jeep-mounted TOW missile. "Remember," the twenty-year veteran reminds the frightened group of armor recruits, "the infantryman is the tank's worst enemy!"

A centurion MBT battalion charges enemy M-60s. The Centurion is the elder statesman in the Armor Corps's inventory, but with a new engine, improved 105mm gun, and reactive armor, it will remain a potent weapon into the next century.

Unlike the paratroops who end basic training with a rousing forced march, or certain naval units who complete training with pomp and ceremony, tank soldiers end their three months of basic training with a visit to Latrun. Latrun is located halfway between Jerusalem and Tel Aviv, its rolling hills adorned with a plush harvest. In the 1948 fighting, however, Latrun was hell on earth — a battlefield for a desperate Jewish military effort against the tenacious warriors of King Abdallah's Arab Legion. Thousands of men on both sides were killed and wounded in ferocious fighting for control of this vital crossroad on the road to Jerusa-lem. Today, Latrun is home to the memory of the 4,650 Israeli tank soldiers who have fallen in the past six wars. Above the old road to Jerusalem via Ramla, a giant concrete stand holding an M4 Sherman overlooks the old fort being converted into the IDF Armored Corps memorial; it is here that new "tank-ists" come in solemn pilgrimage. With an honor

guard, and an eternal flame placed symbolically in an empty battle helmet, the tank soldiers stand and salute the names of the 4,650 engraved on a memorial wall, while a senior officer delivers the standard inspiring speech. It is a ceremony that allows the old guard of the Armored Corps to pass the flame of responsibility to the next generation; more often than not, it is their own sons. It was at Latrun that twice-decorated legendary Brig. Gen. Avigdor Kahalani of "Valley of Tears" fame handed the reins to his son, and where another famous tank soldier, Maj. Gen. Yossi Peled (at the time of this book's writing, the Northern Command commander), watched his son head from basic training to the Armored Corps. HEYL SHIRION is truly a family of fighters!

For thirty years, the IDF's Tank School was located at "Julis," an army camp in the middle of nowhere, "somewhere" in southern Israel. The school was a legendary component of IDF folklore, where simple riflemen third class learned how to fire a 105mm gun, load a heavy shell in haste, and drive a sixty-ton tank. Julis was one of the IDF's greatest successes, producing such brilliant tank soldiers as Avigdor Kahalani, "Yanush" Ben-Gal, and Eli Geva, as well as thousands of silent heroes who helped the Armored Corps to hold off vastly superior Egyptian and Syrian forces. The IDF Tank School's greatest call to fame was a mysterious figure called the "White Horse" — the base master sergeant whose fanatic zeal for discipline instilled more fear in the hearts of generations of tank soldiers than the hordes of RPG-wielding Syrian commandos crawling over the border. Every tank soldier had to survive this white-haired, tyrannical NCO, along with the eighteen-hour days at Julis. HEYL SHIRION earned the reputation of the heartless, insensitive branch of the IDF. But Julis had some

The Centurion MBT, known by its nickname of SHO'T or "whip."

One of the favorite tasks of the tank soldier — maintenance! The job is especially enjoyable when your MERKAVA has been on the firing range on a muddy day!

problems: the facility was cramped, and it was a long trip from the vast, empty spaces of the Negev Desert, where the tank students were brought for their gunnery and riding exercises. So, tradition was shattered; the base was moved, and Julis became a distant memory.

The new "Kalman Magan IDF Tank School" is the largest of all IDF bases. It is located smack in the middle of the Negev Desert, where many of the soldiers often remark that "even if the base didn't have a perimeter fence, there still isn't anything nearby worth escaping to!" Yet why would they want to escape? Air-conditioned barracks have replaced the cramped Julis tents, and state-of-the-art training facili-

ties have replaced antiquated classrooms that were obsolete even when new. Comfort aside, Tank School still means work, and lots of it. For eight to fourteen weeks, the easiest day any tank student can hope for is eighteen hours of classroom study, field training, and harsh physical combat instruction in the "invigorating" atmosphere of the base's 100°F average temperature.

Once through the gates of the Tank School, each soldier proceeds with his education in a particular task, either driver, loader, or gunner. The individual soldier will have absolutely no say as to whether he will be shifting gears, loading shells into a breach, or aiming the 105mm cannon and taking credit for a kill. He also has no say as to the tank unit to which he'll be attached, and in which tank he'll serve. Obviously everyone wants MERKAVAS, but many will have to settle for the M-60s and Centurions in which their fathers might have fought; some might even be unfortunate enough to get TIRANIM — upgraded and up-gunned T-54s, T-55s, and T-62s captured from the Arabs.

The unequivocal master of the world's fleet of main battle tanks, the indigenous MERKAVA or "chariot tank," was born out of the French arms embargo against Israel following the 1967 War. France's move caused Israel to realize that her supply of precious weaponry could no longer depend on fickle allies. It was the catalyst for the production of the KFIR C-2 fighter plane, as well as the MERKAVA. Whereas in the past, Israel had purchased weapons from the inven-

Commanding the only way he knows how, standing upright in his turret perch, an M-60 commander directs his platoon's tanks in a unified assault.

tory of allied arsenals, it now began to produce items to meet their own specific needs. And that is indeed the MERKAVA.

Designed by one of the architects of the IDF Armored Corps, Maj. Gen. Yisrael Tal, the MERKAVA incorporated all the experience of Israeli tank combat. All tanks must have a combination of three principal elements — firepower, protection, and mobility. Yet whereas many armies opt for tanks that have large-caliber guns or high speeds, General Tal knew the IDF sensitivity to casualties, and he wanted an MBT in which the crews could survive. As a result, the MERKAVA was engineered in a unique, low slope design, with an almost vertical front hull. If that configuration doesn't help in deflecting antitank rounds, then the 900-horsepower engine placed up front will stop almost anything flying straight toward it. The MERKAVA is an enormous vehicle, more than twenty-four feet long and twelve feet wide, weighing more than sixty-six tons when fully equipped for battle. Its main armament is the lethal 105mm gun, which over the past twenty-one years has destroyed literally thousands of Arab tanks. Realizing that one of the MERKAVA's greatest adversaries is the missile-wielding infantryman, three 7.62mm light machine guns, and a 52mm or a 60mm, are mounted on the turret. The MERKAVA also has room in the rear to ferry up to five fully equipped infantrymen. Although the MERKAVA's maximum speed is only thirty miles an hour, many tank commanders wryly joke that if it were any faster, the IDF would receive speeding tickets en route to Damascus or Beirut!

In Lebanon, the MERKAVA was a brilliant success, even out-battling Syrian T-72s, the most modern Soviet tank ever to be engaged in actual combat. Although numerous MERKAVAs suffered direct hits, ranging from RPG-7s to point-blank shots from the T-72's powerful 125mm gun, not one crewman died in combat. The success of the MERKAVA led to an Mk. II version, with an even mightier Mk. III under development. Comfortable and roomy when compared to other MBTs, especially the cramped and claustrophobic Soviet tanks, the MERKAVA has a host of technologically advanced fire-control systems that allow its crews to concentrate on battle. A tank is only as good as its crew, and IDF crews are the best.

From day one in the Armored Corps, each soldier undergoes a series of "psychotechnical" examinations, and intense psychological interviews by Armored Corps psychiatrists, to determine his most suitable task. The most prestigious is gunner, second is driver, with loader last. Not everyone can be a gunner, however, and those selected for other tasks must cope. Fresh out of a particularly harsh winter's basic training complete with a mud-soaked fifty-kilometer march, and two weeks keeping the peace in the Nablus *casbah*, Private Itzik had hoped he'd be selected for a gunner's course in a MERKAVA. Unfortunately, the army psychiatrists deemed him "ideal" driver material for a Patton. "At first I was deeply disappointed," smiles Itzik, "but when I sat in control of the M-60 for the first time and was allowed to push the throttle down, I knew I had found my calling!" His fellow platoon mates seem just as eager to sit at the controls of a Teledyne Continental AVDS-1790-2A twelve-cylinder air-cooled diesel engine!

A tank student sometimes will sit in the classroom for ten hours a day, but studies really aren't boring when your instructor is a curvaceous brunette with a knockout smile. Women have been Armored Corps instructors since the dark days of the 1973 Yom Kippur War, when all the available *man*power was rushed to the tank killing ground of the Sinai Desert and Golan Heights to counter Egyptian, Syrian, and even Cuban tank forces. The female soldiers were incorporated into the ranks as a last resort, but it proved to be a blessing in disguise. In the fourteen years since,

What every tank needs — a woman at the helm! With her golden curls escaping her ballistic crewman's helmet, a MERKAVA instructor orders her vehicle into position.

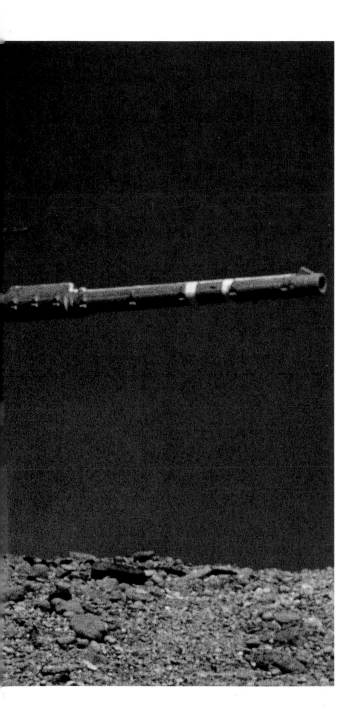

they have proven to be outstanding instructors and highly disciplined soldiers, responsible for the improvement and expansion of the Armored Corps into a professional force. They also have brought to the Armored Corps a human element unmatched in importance. The sight of nail polish on crew helmets and the scent of perfume amid a sea of diesel fuel has helped to sensitize a corps known for its steel and gritty personality. The women are compassionate teachers, who *demand* total concentration and the dedication of their pupils, but don't torture them with mindless punishments as is the norm in basic training. The women teach everything there is to know about being a tank soldier — how to drive, how to shoot, even how to overhaul an engine. In the past few years, one of the most important classes has become the venerable .50-caliber machine gun and its deadly role as an antiaircraft weapon.

During Israel's 1982 invasion of Lebanon, the tank soldier discoverd a new nemesis — the antitank helicopter. For years, it had been universally accepted that one of the greatest threats to a tank was the infantryman. Yet on a sunny June morning in the Lebanese Beka'a Valley, a convoy of Israeli armor from the elite BARAK Brigade was advancing confidently deeper into the Lebanese heartland when a beating noise over the horizon caught their attention. Before the MERKAVA and Centurion commanders standing upright in their turrets had a chance to locate the suspicious noise with their field glasses, or respond with a trigger finger on their cupola-mounted 50-caliber machine guns, the telltale swish of HOT antitank missiles was heard. Within moments, explosions, flames, and the cries of the wounded filled the air. The successful Syrian deployment of French-made Gazelle helicopters fitted with the deadly HOT mis-

A MERKAVA MK.II MBT, the cutting edge of Israel's armor might, heads into defensive firing position.

siles proved traumatic for the Israeli tanker, especially since the Gazelles were able to fire their HOTs out of range of the turret-mounted machine guns. In the ensuing tank battles in Lebanon, the Syrians threw an even mightier airborne nemesis against Israeli armor — the Soviet Mi-24 Hind. The fifty-five-foot-long armored chopper carries a virtual arsenal of anti-tank weaponry, including a four-barreled 12.7mm Gatling gun, 57mm rocket pods, and tubes for firing the deadly Sagger AT-3 missile. Its sighting brought panic into the hearts of the conscript Israeli tankers. The Israelis responded in kind by deploying Hughes Defender-500 and Bell-209 attack helicopters against Syrian armor. The dangerous precedent had been struck, however, and as a result, all tank soldiers from driver to loader must now learn to accurately fire a .50-caliber machine gun at a high angle, as well as the "routine" firing of a 105mm cannon at low trajectory.

Tank School, with all its discipline and pressure, is but an eight- to ten-week stepping-stone on the way to becoming a tank soldier. The long hours in the classroom, the company exercises, the occasional security duty inside the "Green Line" (the West Bank and Gaza) or along the Lebanese frontier, and the intensive training produce a soldier who is not expert in the art of tank warfare, but is equipped with the basics. He is prepared for the next and perhaps most challenging phase of service in HEYL SHIRION — operational assignment. This is known as TZA'MA'P, the Hebrew acronym for "crewman-platoon-company," perhaps best described as the Armor Corps' "finishing school." Here, in the battalion, the young soldier will complete his remaining thirty months of active service; he'll learn the difference between classroom theory and the realities of the field.

Attached to a crew of well-seasoned veterans, the new gunner, driver, or loader will undergo on-the-job training in the battalion's methods of operation, communications, and combat drill. Tank School and TZA'MA'P training are two worlds apart. If a gunner in Tank School was allowed by an understanding female instructor to miss his target during practice, in the battalion, his cynical platoon commander won't permit a less-than-perfect accuracy record, because his abilities can make or break the platoon in battle. If in Tank School the soldier was judged by his grades, in TZA'MA'P he'll be judged solely on performance by the harshest critics he shall ever face — his crew.

The tank crew is without question the tightest knit family in the IDF. In a typical three-year career uninterrupted by war, the four crewmen will spend almost 6,000 hours together inside the cramped world of a tank. They'll have to get used to each other's odors, personalities, and mannerisms. They'll learn to operate as a fine-tuned machine, ready to battle the enemy until ordered to stop. In command of this entire conglomerate is the tank commander, usually a nineteen- to twenty-year-old sergeant, mature beyond his years. The tank commander initiates each new crewman to his beloved tank (more often than not named, christened, and cherished) with the patience of a new father and the harshness of a high-strung Prussian officer. The tank commander knows what it's like to be the "new one" to a vehicle, and what it takes to get through it. First Sergeant Dani is a natural for tanks. The twenty-year-old native of the "sun and fun" Red Sea city of Eilat has the compact physical stature that made tanks the only viable option after an ear infection made submarine service an impossibility. An outstanding graduate of Tank School and Tank Commander's School, First Sergeant Dani sees his responsibility for molding the crew as the most important aspect of his job. No sacrifice is too great to insure a successful crew, including spending long hours into the night helping a new gunner familiarize himself with the battalion's unique firing orders, codes, and battle contingencies. "It's not only the good feeling of having a crew whose friendship makes the three years pass easier, but when war breaks out, if we can't operate together, chances are we'll die together!"

The high rate of attrition among tank soldiers in combat is a constant thought in the minds of Armored Corps commanders. HEYL SHIRION's commanders and planners have done almost everything imaginable to maximize a crew's chances for survival, safety, and comfort. These range from the boxes of ''Blazer'' reactive armor fitted to the M-60s and Centurions, and the ingenious conceptual design of the MERKAVA MBT, to the special web gear that includes ammunition pouches worn on the chest and long rectangular canteens that make sitting inside the tank in full battle gear a more comfortable experience. It seems that no expense is too great for the Armored Corps in

Patton MBTs deploy for battle during an exercise in southern Israel.

preparing their men for the inevitable, but sometimes corners can be cut. In the past few years, one of the most effective and technologically advanced methods of training has been the coveted ''one day simulator.'' This is a video game with quite realistic overtones — shells costing $15,000 can be fired without actually costing a cent, and a tank can travel thousands of kilometers without drinking a drop of diesel fuel!

Located at the ancient Armored Corps school at Julis, the futuristic simulator offers a wide array of training possibilities to every tank brigade in the IDF. Whereas a regular tank crew might have the opportunity to cross an AVLB (armored vehicle launched bridge) only once a year during large-scale maneuvers, the simulator allows the driver to cross dozens of bridges without the risk of capsizing his vehicle. The simulator is versatile: Battalion commanders are offered a menu of simulated options so they can choose which particular aspect deserves the greatest emphasis. A major who wants, for example, to condition his men for service in the desert might choose a program that allows for driving and firing on "sandy conditions." The simulator is also very realistic. The driver's perch is a one-to-one replica of the real thing, as is the gunner's seat. Next door sits the examiner, a female NCO who has additional NBC (nuclear, biological, and chemical warfare) experience, as well as insight into modes of infantry attack. The examiners will formulate thousands of different scenarios for thousands of different soldiers, from third-week conscripts to thirty-year reservist veterans.

This is the first time for Shai in the simulator. The nineteen-year-old corporal was lucky enough to have been selected as a driver to one of the more elite armor units on the Golan Heights, but first he must confront the imagination of Aliza, the simulator examiner. Sitting by her computer command center, Aliza nestles comfortably in her chair; she adjusts her headphones and ex-PLO "wooly pully" sweater and assumes the role of tank commander. Today's scenario is the Negev Desert, and Aliza orders Shai to commence his advance. "Forward . . . forward, increase your speed a bit." On the monitor, Shai observes his movement and recalls happier days play-

"The thick sand-gray line!" Minutes before H-hour, reservists prepare their up-armored and up-gunned M-60 MBTs for battle.

ing video games, when Aliza breaks into his thoughts to inform him of a small AVLB in the distance. "Head left . . . straighten yourself out on the bridge . . . shift a few degrees to the right . . . slowly . . . slowly, I said. Nicely done." As the simulation continues, Shai succumbs to the pressure of performing well for Aliza, and for his battalion OC, who will receive his score. As he wipes the sweat from his brow, quickly so as not to leave his controls for an instant, the advance into the computerized desert continues. Soon, however, Shai enters a mine field and an ambush. "Bear left . . . left . . . you're entering a mine field . . . quickly . . . incoming enemy fire . . . ," and then a loud explosion and the driver's perch shakes and rattles. Shai has moved directly into a desert plain filled with Russian-made antitank mines. "You're on a mine . . . carry out the exfiltration maneuver now . . . now!" Shai's loss of control over the tank is finalized when Aliza's understanding "OK . . . turn off your engine" is heard over the headphones.

No matter how cost effective and diverse the simulator is, it can never hope to replace the real thing, and the closest one can get to the real thing is on a volcanic plateau called the Golan Heights. While the Lebanese frontier has fanatic *Hizballah* "martyr material" just waiting for the chance to cross the border and blow themselves up, and the Jordanian frontier might have the odd Palestinian terrorist looking for a breach in the fence, Israeli soldiers stationed on the Golan face a more compelling threat — 4,000 Syrian T-74s, T-72s, T-62s, and T-54s/55s which have Israel in their gun sights!

Yet at a tank base close to the Syrian lines, life continues as usual. The smell of diesel fuel fills the air, as does the incessant clanking of maintenance — "oh forever maintenance." The barracks are small aluminum excuses for a hut, which house up to eight soldiers. Life in the Armored Corps is isolated and harsh. While the "spoiled" paratroopers might get weekend leave three weeks out of four, a tanker is

lucky if he gets home once in a new moon. Discipline is strict, the work hard and heavy, and the threat of combat very real. To lighten the spartan atmosphere, the female company clerks plant flowers, an occasional pop singer is brought around for entertainment, and the men have even tried to raise money to buy a color television for the "rec room" by selling sodas and fresh-baked pita bread to motorists on the road. The rooms may be decorated with posters of Samantha Fox, and rock tunes may be playing on the radio, but amenities are few. A Syrian vehicle recognition chart on the door, loose 5.56mm cartridges rolling around the floor, and cigarette smoke thick enough to hide an armored division — this is the reality of serving on the heights!

Guarding the heights means war is but seconds away, and the tankers live twenty-four hours a day in a high state of alert. Alert means sleeping in your Nomex coveralls, with your GLILON rifle substituting for a warm girl, and wearing boots instead of slippers. An alarm means a ghastly siren, which causes each soldier to leap out of bed, pat the barrack's black-bereted watermelon mascot, and run toward his vehicle, adjusting his flak vest and web gear, in time that would make an Olympic sprinter blush. The soldiers leap aboard the vehicles, open hatches, and check systems, and in a matter of moments the engines of the MERKAVAS are ignited and each soldier's psyche is prepared for combat. The tension is intense inside the tank. The "alarm" will usually end with the commander telling his men just how long it took them to get ready. But the men never know whether an exercise is just an exercise until they're in the tanks. The next time, instead of their commander's familiar voice, they just might hear the roar of F-15s and the whine of incoming shells, and have the opportunity to find out if their Nomex suits are really fire retardant!

Reaching his tank in record time during an alarm is not the tank soldier's only chance to prove his worth. Once a year HEYL SHIRION celebrates "Armored Corps Day," with the festivities marked by an impressive competition among the best conscript tank units in the corps in the tank's "six golden tasks" —*long-range firing; short-range firing; quick firing exercise; battlefield maneuvering, engagement, and deployment; field stripping and assembly of .50-caliber and 7.62mm machine guns;* and *spreading out the treads.* It's generally a joyous occasion, marked by fun, smiles, picnics, and a visit from the top brass. Armored Corps Day 1988 was special, however. It was HEYL SHIRION's fortieth anniversary, and indeed they had something to be proud of. They had grown from only two antiquated Cromwell tanks donated by two defecting British servicemen in 1948, to a 4,000-plus-tank armada equipped with the world's best battle tanks, and manned by the world's most battle-ready crews. Armored Corps Day 1988 also, and ironically, fell on the exact day that, fifteen years ago, thousands of Syrian tanks crossed the cease-fire line to initiate the Yom Kippur War. That coincidence was heavy on the heart of Armor Corps commander Brigadier General Ben-Hanan as he viewed the BARAK Brigade's performance in the festivities: That date also marked the fifteenth anniversary of his war against the Syrians, and the Sagger missile that nearly ended his life.

One would think that the firing accuracy contests would be the most dramatic event of the competition, but the favorite is "spreading out the treads." As the top brass looks on attentively on a sunny field on the Golan Heights, a BARAK crew armed only with their tools, flak vests, and smiles completes this grueling maintenance routine on their MERKAVA in an astounding four minutes and twenty seconds. Unfortunately, their exhaustive performance is marked by rousing applause from a unit of the SA'AR Brigade, who had just completed the same maneuver on their MERKAVA in four minutes and twelve seconds! The contest continues as the various brigade commanders anxiously watch from a command tent. The colonels, majors, and even brigadier generals act as nervous parents observing a Little League game, wagering a few shekels here and there on their men "who had

better not lose"! At 1600, the victory trophy is presented to BARAK Brigade commander Colonel B., whose face explodes in a smile from ear to ear. It's the second consecutive year that BARAK has won the Armored Corps Day contest, and the BARAK crews offer "war cries" of pride to their victorious commander. At day's end, Brigadier General Ben-Hanan offers some personal insight by saying "the contest is the nicest victory act possible to honor those who fought and died here fifteen years ago."

And so it goes on the Golan Heights for the brave men of the Armored Corps. The routine of service in the modern age's "steel cavalry" continues uninterrupted. Patrols are mounted along the border, alerts are warned, and intensive exercises are carried out as though they were the real thing. The paratroopers might enjoy the limelight of the "elite," but when push comes to shove, and the diplomats fail in their tasks, it will be the black berets who will face the oncoming onslaught and insure that "METZADA will never fall a second time."

The old guard meets the new. Chief Armored Corps Officer Brig. Gen. Yossi Ben-Hanan, a hero of the 1967 and 1973 wars, reviews a graduating class of Tank School.

Chapter 6
Combined Arms: GOLANI Brigade and the MERKAVA

Mt. Hermon is a fantastic symbol of majestic beauty in the war-torn Middle East. Known in Arabic by the affectionate name *Jebel es-Shiekh,* "Mountain of the Old Man," because of its snowy peaks, the towering mountain is an irony: The seemingly peaceful rise acts as a crossroads to Lebanon, Syria, and Israel. The mountain's two peaks offer both the Syrians and Israelis excellent bird's-eye views of each other, and both sides maintain heavily fortified electronic intelligence-gathering posts atop their respective summits. This incessant vigilance is with great justification. In all probability, the next major Arab-Israeli flare-up will be between the IDF and the Syrian Army. With a peace treaty with the Egyptians still valid, and with relative peace along the border with Jordan, the volatile Golan Heights becomes the most logical scenario for any future war. It would be the most brutal combat in the Middle East's bloody history.

To insure that the IDF is taking its military prowess seriously, the Syrians have worked at a feverish pace to upgrade their offensive military potential. During the 1973 Yom Kippur War, the Syrians launched a five-division blitzkrieg across the "purple line" (the border separating the two belligerents). They fought hard, fought well, and almost retook the Golan Heights, and possibly much of northern Israel. During the 1982 War in Lebanon, the IDF faced the Syrian

Leading the way and kicking up dust, mine-clearing M-60s clear a path for NA'HA'L infantrymen, following close behind.

Where it starts for every Israeli infantryman. At the Wailing Wall in Jerusalem GOLANI recruits swear their oath of allegiance to God, to Israel, and to the IDF.

Army once again in battle. Although the Syrian Air Force performed miserably, losing all her Lebanon SAM sites and more than ninety MiGs, Sukhois, and attack helicopters, her tank and commando forces fought tenaciously, and with admirable skill and courage. Today, the Syrian Army is the second most powerful military force in the Middle East, and is aiming hard for parity with the IDF. It has a 350,000-man standing army, six armored divisions complete with 1,200 of the latest Soviet T-72s as well as T-62s and T-55s, SAM batteries, and almost 100 SCUD, FROG, SS-12, and SS-21 surface-to-surface missiles capable of hitting any target in Israel. To all observers, Syria seems highly capable of achieving her ultimate military objective — the recapture of the 780-square-mile volcanic plateau known as the Golan Heights, an ultrastrategic piece of real estate that has already cost the lives of thousands of Syrian and Israeli combatants.

A majority of the Israeli soldiers who died atop the heights were either tank soldiers attached to the 7th and 188th BARAK Armored Brigades, or infantrymen from the 1st GOLANI Brigade. For the tankers, 1973 was their year of decision. With the defense of the Golan spread between the 7th Armored Brigade in the northern sector and the 188th in the south, the thinly spaced line was hammered by a Syrian blitzkrieg unprecedented in its ferocity. The 188th was hit hardest, and in a matter of hours ceased to exist. With most of its vehicles destroyed and commanders dead, including brigade commander Col. Yitzhak Ben-Shoham, the Syrian advance seemed unstoppable. Then a lone Israeli maverick appeared. His name was Capt. Tzvi Greengold, and his lone Centurion tank, which soon entered military folklore as "Force Tzvika," waged a private and highly remarkable war, holding the Syrian armor until help from the reservists reached the front.

In the northern sector, Col. Yanush Ben-Gal's elite 7th Armored Brigade had prepositioned itself on defensive ridges, affording excellent firing positions onto the advancing Syrian armor. The brigade's Centurion MBT's accurate 105mm guns and highly trained crews fought off five times their numbers in the epic battle of the "Valley of Tears." The fighting was fierce, and often at close-quarter range, with tanks battling one another only yards apart. Days later when the reservist formations reached the fighting, the 7th Armored Brigade had lost a majority of its fighters, and every one of its tanks had been hit at least once. Nevertheless, the brigade survived long enough to save the front, and northern Israel.

The GOLANI Infantry Brigade has an extensive history of action against the Syrians on the Golan. The first conventional infantry unit formed by the HAGANAH in 1947, the 1st GOLANI Brigade fought in the north against Syrian, Iraqi, and Lebanese forces in the 1948 War, as well as captured the port of Eilat. Soon after, the brigade became something of an IDF trash bag, absorbing a disproportional share of new immigrants who flocked to the Israeli shores in the 1950s. The brigade stood tall, and its highly motivated officers transformed GOLANI into a crack, fully operational unit defending northern Israel. In 1967, the GOLANI Brigade was the vanguard of the assault up the Golan Heights' steep cliffs. Its tenacity under murderous Syrian fire led to the capture of the heights, even though it was defended by thirteen heavily fortified fortresses. The hardest fought of all was Tel-Fahar. It took two GOLANI battalions and almost thirty dead to neutralize the Syrian "monster." Dozens of its soldiers were awarded bravery medals, most of them posthumously. Tel-Fahar is now a GOLANI landmark, and all GOLANI recruits are taken to it, much as pilgrims journey to a holy shrine.

Six years later, GOLANI was entrusted with the defense of the Golan Heights, and they bore the brunt of the Syrian onslaught. They manned a series of lightly held forward firing positions, which were defended with fanatic zeal. One such position was the "old man" himself, *Jebel es-Shiekh*, Mount Hermon. It was also the only Israeli position to fall on the

Golan. Defended by only *thirteen* GOLANI infantrymen, the invaluable intelligence-gathering post was assaulted by the elite of the Syrian armed forces, her 82d Paratroop Brigade. In a heliborne assault, and after much bitter fighting, the old man, called by many the "eyes of Israel," now flew a Syrian flag. Throughout the remainder of the fighting, GOLANI stood fast, not relinquishing another position even though most of their strongpoints were completely surrounded and under incessant siege. Yet the humiliation of Mount Hermon's capture remained a GOLANI obsession, and attempt after attempt to retake it met with failure and horrendous casualties. Finally, on the last day of the war, the climb began. It was a full brigade effort, and following the hand-to-hand, no-quarter battle, the Israeli and GOLANI flags once again flew atop the Israeli peak. The battle was one of the fiercest in Middle Eastern military history, and resulted in the decimation of many of GOLANI's men, including many battalion and company commanders.

The defense of the heights has become a way of life for the GOLANI and tank soldiers serving the IDF today. For it would most probably be these same two families of fighters who, in a future war, would again fight the Syrians for control of the heights. Yet, in the next round, the Syrians will face a very different IDF than it encountered in 1973. The initial setbacks suffered in the opening shots of the Yom Kippur War taught the IDF the value of consolidating its ground forces under overall and unified commands. The strategic concept is SHILUV KOHOT or "combined arms," and its main players are the tank, infantry, paratroop, engineer, and artillery units molded together in a relatively new concept called "Ground Forces Command," best described as the way the IDF plans to win its next war!

Combined arms entered the IDF vocabulary as a result of lessons learned in 1973. Until that fateful war, IDF units were basically independent of one another — infantry forces didn't have to rely on tank support, and vice versa. This was effective strategy

Desert flowers and RPGs. Preparing for combined GOLANI and tank maneuvers in northern Israel.

when you had your enemy on the run! But 1973 changed everything. The Egyptian and Syrian deployment of infantry tank-killing squads armed with RPG-7s and Saggers, together with tank brigades supported by massive artillery barrages, was a potent punch the IDF could not emulate. Combined arms became a logical stepping-stone from the old battlefield to the missile-saturated environment the IDF knew it would face in the next major conflict. Indeed, Lebanon, and Operation Peace for Galilee, was the combined arms baptism under fire. In brilliant fashion, Israeli infantry, armor, engineer, and artillery units hammered away at their objectives until a hole was punched through and a breakthrough achieved. The GOLANI and armor units fought hard against the Syrians in Lebanon's Beka'a Valley. As always when Israeli and Syrian soldiers met, casualties were high, and every inch of territory was paid for in blood. But combined arms worked.

83

In 1983, the concept of a Ground Corps Command was finally established to consolidate all the elements of combined arms under one umbrella command. Yet while the borders remain relatively tranquil, the Ground Corps Command vigilantly prepares for war, and those preparations mean maneuvers — the IDF's way of teaching the men of the infantry to interact with the machines of the Armored Corps.

In a serene spot somewhere in northern Israel, which shall remain nameless for security reasons, elements of two GOLANI battalions have faithfully gathered. The infantrymen can still recall their first intro-

"TANGERINE PEEL, THIS IS YELLOW RIVER. ACCORDING TO ATTACK PLAN ALEPH, ALL SYSTEMS GO." M-60s fitted with giant wheelers go for the nasty big boys — antiarmor mines.

duction to GOLANI in BA'K'UM, when the brigade's recruitment officer honestly promised that "in GOLANI, you will each see all of Israel . . . with your left foot and your right!" No statement could have been more accurate. In less than one year of service with the brigade, most of these nineteen year olds have already walked thousands of kilometers, over meadows, hills, swamps, and deserts. In the mud, rain, and brutal Middle Eastern sun, they have "toured" much of their country, most of the time in a hearty run, lugging countless kilos of equipment. Yet today, little emphasis will be given to GOLANI's traditional passion for marching. Instead, these GOLANI foot sluggers will concentrate their strengths, initiative, and speed in learning the most necessary lesson of combined arms — how to deploy with and against tanks.

Before the stage can be set for war games, the GOLANI fighters are entitled to a bit of firing practice. Amid the thistles, thorns, and sandy hills, an improvised range has been established, utilizing sandbags and paper targets. Squad after squad "assumes the position," cocks their GLILON assault rifles (a short-barreled version of the GALIL), and shows off the marksmanship they learned in basic. Dutiful attention is given to emptying a few thirty-round GLILON magazines, as well as firing thousands of rounds of 7.62mm ammunition from the squad's support FN MAGs. Yet the purpose of today's gathering is the platoon's anti-tank arsenal of RPG-7s, LAW rockets, Dragon ATGWs (antitank guided weapons), and armor-piercing rifle grenades.

A GOLANI AT squad brings their tripod-supported TOW into firing position.

85

With a camouflaged net providing cover, a GOLANI rifleman creeps into position, awaiting the order to fire.

The platoon's weapons instructor is a feisty sergeant named Rena. It's only been a few years since women soldiers were allowed to become weapons instructors in infantry units, yet they've more than proven their worth. Rena, for example, is one of the best in the brigade and takes great pride when the brigade OC calls her "a Syrian tanker's worst nightmare!" She wears a black-market U.S. Nomex tanker's coveralls, which all but conceal her shapely figure, and an olive bush hat, which hides her dark curls. To add to her "tough" mystique, she goes nowhere and does nothing without her GLILON. Yet this "Rambo" with nail polish is a highly capable weapons instructor, whose patience is exceeded only by her dedication.

Squad after squad of GOLANI fighters eagerly await their chance to stand by Rena and fire the revered RPG-7. Boys will be boys, and the chance to show off in front of their female comrade is rivaled only by their desire to show off in front of the platoon commander, Lieutenant Gidi. A short and stocky fellow with a menacing disposition, Gidi was once one of the brigade's premier snipers, until his call came for officers' course. Taking his attention away from a mountain lizard he has just befriended, Lieutenant Gidi stresses to his assembled faithful that "lives of fellow GOLANI fighters were risked to obtain this 'toy' for you, and they didn't bust their asses so that you lazies can miss!" He then goes on to threaten that "the price of each grenade will be deducted from the monthly salary of each soldier who misses the target." The infantrymen, who will neither see the world nor get rich in the IDF, take this threat seriously, especially when they earn just a little more than $50 U.S. a month. Their target today is the charred remains of a T-34 tank, possibly one captured from Egypt more than thirty years earlier, or one retrieved in Lebanon only days before. The T-34, affectionately nicknamed HAZAKEN or "old man," makes a striking target, 100 yards away from the firing pit.

As the men sit in uncharacteristic patience atop a rocky hill, Sergeant Rena calls her pupils one by one and hands them a launcher and an 85mm PG-7 grenade from a large pile. Although the men have already fired an RPG a dozen or so times, Rena orders each one to recite the firing procedure before being allowed to take aim. Standing at attention, a soldier grabs the launcher and grenade and goes over each step one by one, aloud for all to hear: "SCREW CARDBOARD CYLINDER CONTAINING PROPELLANT TO THE MISSILE. INSERT GRENADE INTO MISSILE LAUNCHER, LINE UP CAP WITH MUZZLE HAMMER. REMOVE NOSE CAP, AND EXTRACT SAFETY PIN. AIM AT TARGET AND FIRE." Only when Sergeant Rena offers her approving smile can the infantryman assume a prone firing position, aim, and pull sharply on the trigger. The blast is deafening, the smoke is suffocating, and the results are exhilarating. Traveling at an average velocity of 300 meters per second, the round hits the

T-34 in the turret and ignites into a wild fireball.

The procession of firing continues enthusiastically. Most soldiers hit their targets, and those who miss can expect a less-than-gentle tap on the helmet by Lieutenant Gidi, who offers a humiliating expression of disgust. When all the RPG grenades are fired, the platoon will switch to the 66mm LAW rocket, then the Dragon, and finally the rifle grenades. It will be a long day of explosions, thuds, and the smell of gunpowder. Night brings a ''short'' ten-kilometer march, which hopefully will get the men up for the ''war'' tomorrow.

Wake-up the following morning is at 0400. After folding away the tents and sleeping bags, the infantry sections head to a brief meal and a weapons' inspection. They are then introduced to their partner for the next few days — the MERKAVA MBT.

GOLANI's mission in this training exercise will be infantry support of the BARAK Brigade's MERKAVAS against a combined defensive force of Centurion and M-60 MBTs from the SA'AR (''Storm'') Brigade. Although in service with the IDF for almost twenty years, the American M-60 has been upgraded for service in the twenty-first century. Its most striking modification has been re-armoring with dozens of cubes of reactive armor. Known by its international name of ''Blazer,'' the reactive armor is literally an add-on exploding box, which destroys an oncoming warhead before it can destroy the tank. It is a typically ingenious Israeli invention, inspired by the long-held IDF armor ethic of crew survivability over maneuverability. In Lebanon, the M-60s and Centurions fitted with the Blazer boxes absorbed numerous antitank hits, saving the lives of hundreds of tank crews. Many Israeli tanks returned to base with their armor boxes detonated, in what otherwise would surely have been an enemy kill! The notion was so successful that the Russians, after ''borrowing'' an M-60 captured by the Syrians, began to equip their new T-80 with ''bootleg'' Blazer armor, much to the chagrin of U.S. tank commanders.

A GOLANI antitank reconnaissance force and their prized weapon: the jeep-mounted TOW missile.

The MERKAVAS deploy for battle in exciting fashion. In what resembles a mechanized version of a cavalry charge of years past, a dozen or so MERKAVAS bristling with antennas, commanders standing upright in their turrets, form a long line of armor might. When the first flare is fired, the engines are ignited, and a monumental cloud of smoke is produced by the charge. The clanking sound of their tracks has a mesmerizing effect on the young infantrymen, in this their first exercise with armor. From inside the bright green aluminum confines of their M113s, the infantrymen can hear only what is transpiring around them. Their fleet of M113s is in close pursuit of the MERKAVA charge, although the choreography of the attack will remain a mystery to them until the first round is fired and their ramps swing open. It's a tense time, as all new experiences are, but the choking dust and bumpy haul make this first entry into battle distasteful at best. Yet before the quick feet of the GOLANI brown

berets can face the Storm Brigade on the field of battle, two integral elements of combined arms will provide an *explosive* opening act — the artillery and combat engineers.

Time was when the F-4E Phantoms, A-4 Sky-hawks, and Mirage IIICs of the Israel Air Force were considered the IDF's "flying artillery," and their fearless pilots were called gunners. So accurate and devastating were the IAF's air strikes against enemy ground targets that the traditional heavy guns of an artillery force seemed to be an unnecessary IDF investment. But then came the War of Attrition, and the large-scale deployment of Soviet surface-to-air missiles,

A platoon commander checks his radioman/grenadier's equipment, as a GOLANI rifleman squad prepares for its turn on the assault course.

electronic countermeasures, and radar-controlled, multibarreled antiaircraft guns. During the 1973 War, these new ground threats not only neutralized the Israeli air effort in the skies, but virtually destroyed the IAF's ability to provide pinpoint ground strikes against enemy troop deployments. Combined arms changed all that, and proved to be HEYL TOTHANIM's (Artillery Corps') renaissance. The IDF's obsolete

With a red-colored smoke grenade informing the IAF Bell-212 pilot of a "cold LZ," supplies are heli-lifted to a mechanized GOLANI force.

Amid the beauty of desert flowers and sun-burnt weeds, GOLANI riflemen advance through the hills of the Golan Heights alongside their mighty MERKAVA.

arsenal of WW II cannons, 155mm guns, and heavy mortars fitted to aging Sherman tanks were replaced by American-made self-propelled artillery pieces such as the M-109 155mm, M-107 175mm, and M-110 203mm. The Artillery Corps also received other goodies, including the U.S. LANCE missile; captured Syrian and Egyptian 130mm guns; Katyusha rockets; and ubiquitous 122mm, 135mm, 240mm, and 290mm battlefield rockets. To be totally integrated into the framework of combined arms, the Artillery Corps would have to develop into a full "front-line combat corps," much like the armor and infantry. The big guns could no longer expect to operate from their "safe" positions in the rear; instead they'd have to assume an "at-the-front" ground-support role, providing massive fire support for the attacking tanks and infantrymen. Lebanon was their first test.

One of the most striking images of Israel's 1982

invasion of Lebanon was the M-109 batteries firing point-blank into the urban Beirut quagmire. Lebanon was a tough war for the IDF, but particularly brutal for the artillery gunners. Ordered to eliminate PLO targets in a combat scenario where enemy fortifications and civilian dwellings were one and the same, the gunners faced an often-agonizing dilemma of professional duty and moral consciousness. The "no clear-cut identifiable enemy" also had its effects in the rear, where the gunners had to maintain a supreme vigilance against guerrilla attacks and acts of sabotage.

Today, the IDF artilleryman is a full-fledged combatant. He serves as an infantryman along the Lebanese frontier, conducts security details inside the Green Line, and of course, is expected to provide accurate and unrelenting artillery support. For these exercises, dozens of artillery batteries have been assembled, ranging from reservists manning ex-North

Korean/ex-PLO BM-11 Katyusha rockets, to conscripts from an M-109 battery, GIMEL (3d) Battery, who just completed a "for-what-seemed-like-a-lifetime" month-long stint along the Lebanese frontier. Participation in these exercises means a wondrous change from the "mud and fun" of the Lebanese frontier.

Service in an artillery battery is almost identical to that of the tank soldier. A twelve-week basic infantry training routine is followed by a professions course, which is followed by "finishing school" in the respective battalion. Also like service with tanks, an artillery crew becomes a close-knit family, and like most IDF close-knit families, the crew spends a good portion of its "together time" performing mundane vehicle maintenance. GIMEL Battery is no different. The crew spends countless hours checking, strengthening, and cleaning the treads; checking, double-checking, and even triple-checking fire controls; oiling all moving parts; tightening thousands of bolts; and performing the Artillery Corps' version of a three-man circus — six sets of biceps frantically thrusting a cleaning rod through the 155mm gun's barrel. The battery's strict commander, First Lieutenant Eli, a product of one of the IDF's most difficult professional officer courses, is a workaholic who is awake more than twenty hours a day — going over charts, checking the equipment, examining the DAVID fire control computer, and seeing to the needs of his men. "El," as he is called by his men, knows that at a moment's notice, his crew can awaken from their comfortable sleeping bags, remove the camouflage netting from his vehicle, load their first forty-three kilo shells into the gun's breech, and be awaiting the order to fire. The crew on the other hand has collectively given up on sleep

for the remainder of this exercise; they will concentrate solely on HITTING THE INTENDED TARGET! Sergeant Udi is quick to say of his crew efforts: "When we hear over the radio that we hit our mark, our big bang was worth it!"

Another group of soldiers who are an essential component of combined arms is the underrated though forcefully proud combat engineers. Much like the Artillery Corps, the combat engineers traditionally had taken a back seat to the combat exploits of the infantry-type units. During the War of Attrition, combat engineers built the now-infamous Bar-Lev Line along the Suez Canal, and built the bridges across the Suez Canal under unrelenting bombardment during the 1973 War. The war's aftermath and the evolution of combined arms into the IDF vocabulary meant a new mission for the mine-cleaners, bridge-layers, and sappers. They were to become "shock" troops — the first ones on the battlefield, to prepare it for the eventual advance of armor and infantry units.

With the combat engineers, the word *combat* was stressed, as engineer units attached to different divisions and task forces would become independent mechanized and infantry forces, fighting on their own to achieve specific military tasks. They were also to become masters at NBC countermeasures, a more-than-prophetic task considering the Syrians have shown such recent interest in chemical warfare, and Palestinian terrorists are rumored to be producing "chemical terrorist bombs." In Lebanon the combat engineers also had to contend with thousands of tons of precarious unexploded ordnance, as well as defuse a new enemy — booby-trap devices. All in all, the combat engineers have adapted their abilities in perfect fashion to carry out their destined combined arms roles.

For all intents and purposes, the soldiers of HANDA-SAH KRAVIT (combat engineers) are full-fledged infantrymen who have the added skills to destroy obstacles, build bridges, defuse unexploded ordnance, and survive a chemical attack. Like the Armored and Artillery

---

Drinking out of his canteen and speaking on the radio while wearing his gas mask, a combat engineer demonstrates one of his Corps' principal tasks — helping other units survive the effects of an NBC attack.

Paratroopers in their gas masks race through a "chemical attack" consisting of an eerie yellow simulation cloud.

Corps, the combat engineers is not a voluntary service, but in recent years, thousands have requested to fill its ranks. They undergo an intense infantry basic training almost identical to that of the paratroops and GO-LANI and GIVA'ATI infantry brigades, which is followed by professions courses in the corps' seven specialized fields: *demolition* and *mining; armored engineering, fording,* and *bridge-laying; bomb disposal; construction, fortifications,* and *road-building; heavy mechanical construction equipment; camouflage* and *engineering deception;* and lastly, and perhaps most importantly in the past few years, *defense against atomic, bacteriological,* and *chemical warfare.*

For this "simulated" battlefield, the role assigned to this anonymous engineer battalion is simple: Break a wide hole through a zone "full of antipersonnel and antitank mines"! This delicate and once time-consuming task will begin by firing a large rocket fitted with explosive tails, which will punch a gap through the mine field, allowing the engineers to spread out and work in a more effective manner. Watching the mine-clearing experts work is like a lesson in self-motivation. The combat engineers are without a doubt the most gung ho combat unit around. They carry out each assignment as if the survival of the state depended on it, and they take great pains to always carry on their person the sign of unit pride — the gray beret. Riding into the middle of the mine-field labyrinth in the speeding wake of a NAGMASHOT (a heavily armored and armed APC made out of a Centurion's chassis and customized for the combat engineer's use), the gray berets tackle their task with a host of specialized equipment, ranging from elec-

tronic sensors to specially designed rectangular-shaped antimine shoes, which allow the soldier to walk on a suspected area without inflicting enough pressure on the earth to detonate a mine. In maneuvers such as this, the work is tedious. In wartime, it is highly dangerous and must be carried out in haste. As Captain Yuval, a twenty-seven-year-old company commander who as a sergeant in 1982 cleared hundreds of "very real" Palestinian mine fields in Leba-

Combat engineer sappers wear anti-pressure "snow boots" for a stroll through a minefield.

non, says with pride: "If it wasn't highly dangerous, extremely difficult, and very urgent, the brigade commanders would use their own sapper forces. We are highly trained, *extremely* motivated, and capable of clearing any and every mine field we'll be called upon to remove. We do it with guts and determination, and soon, when we're issued portable field computers, which will allow us to predict mine-field layouts, we'll do it with technology!"

It's almost 0500, time for these war games to commence. Northern Israel's tranquil morning haze has been shattered by a barrage from the rapid-firing M-109 155mm batteries. A two-company-sized force of mechanized combat engineers (gray berets *faithfully* placed in trouser cargo pockets) has blasted through and cleaned a path through the "mine fields" and natural obstacles for their advancing armor, as well as prepared contingency deployments in case of an NBC attack. The GOLANI infantrymen have all had a chance to lace up their boots, clean their weapons, and recheck their equipment. The preliminaries of battle have been completed, and it's time now for the tanks to take center stage.

When the MERKAVAS enter the firing field, a host of targets appear to the tank commanders. When the commanders shout their orders, drivers drive, loaders load their AP shells, and gunners aim. It is a well-rehearsed exercise in destruction that has been mastered to split-second accuracy. In the Armored Corps, a good tank crew will hit a target within the first four shots. Since this target is a mere three hundred yards into the site, the lead MERKAVA's commander, First Sergeant Dani, tells his men that the brigade OC is watching, and they had better hit the target on the first try.

Seconds later, the order to fire is given. The roar of the 105mm cannon letting loose its deadly round is a deafening explosion heard miles away. It is so loud, in fact, that the top brass and brigade representatives in a command tent a kilometer away have all covered their ears. Then their hands are busy applauding: Sergeant Dani's tank has turned a lifeless hulk

of steel into a blazing inferno on the first shot. Sergeant Dani's vehicle is blanketed with such a thick coat of kicked-up dust that the sergeant looks like a photographic negative, with white hair, eyebrows, and mustache. Although the blinding cloud of dust and smoke distorts his vision, he knows from the sounds that he has hit his target, so he fires a dozen or so bursts from his cupola-mounted .50-caliber machine gun for good measure. It's his tank's version of a victory dance. Dozens of other MERKAVAS now begin firing at their respective targets. War, on this field in northern Israel, is underway.

The roar of the 105mm gun is GOLANI's invitation to the party. The M113s' rear ramps open slowly; before they can hit the earth the infantrymen are out of their APCs and racing for position. The officers and NCOs have been instructed to work their ranks hard, as the last three months of patrolling in Gaza have made the battalion sluggish. There are no stone-throwing youths and rubber bullets here, just your web gear, your GLILON, and your squad.

GOLANI's initial performance is good. The men appear to be up for the exercise, and follow their officers and NCOs with zeal. They perform all the assault techniques as trained, and enjoy the opportunity to fire their weapons into the cliff of a nearby hill. Dozens of calls to "follow me" are heard as the men are led into battle. As in real combat, they will have to overcome and defeat all the true battlefield elements. Their feet will carry them over the unrelenting terrain, mine fields and obstacles will be breached by the battalion's sapper company, and, as is painfully evident, their gas masks will get them through a poison gas attack. Years ago, the IDF never took seriously the threat of gas warfare, that is until the Iraqis and Iranians began using it with such murderous vigor. The Syrians also have begun an arms race in chemical weapons, and no one doubts their resolve to use such agents of destruction. It is a fact very much on the minds of the GOLANI conscripts as they place gas masks over their faces. Adjusting the mask is difficult amid the thunderous explosions, choking dust, and shouted orders. War, even in game form, has a fair degree of finality to it, however, and the masks are attended to quickly.

As the conventional battle is fought, and the mechanized GOLANI elements head into the SA'AR force's antitank trenches for a little "enemy purification," another distinctive GOLANI force goes into action. A force of dedicated tank hunters in jeeps and M113s, equipped primarily with the deadly American TOW missile, race through the northern Israeli hills. The tank hunters outflank the SA'AR armor force to hit them in a wide-flanking movement of tank destruction.

Toward the end of day two of the exercise, the combined GOLANI and MERKAVA force captures its objectives, and the war game is history. The "enemy" M-60 force also performed well, scoring dozens of hits on the range, but was meant only to add realism to the event, not any serious resistance. As a cease-fire is called, the MERKAVA tankers are allowed to leave their behemoth vehicles to undergo a proud review by the division OC, Brigadier General R. For the past forty-eight hours, they have sat inside the 140° F (60° C) saunas, loading, aiming, and pushing gears, and they welcome the chance to allow their perspiration-soaked Nomex coveralls to dry in the outside world's 100+° F (40° C) heat. Brigadier General R. has nothing but compliments for his armada of black berets, and goes over all the technical mistakes, correct moves, and ideas for the future. Meanwhile back at SA'AR's camp, the brigade OC congratulates his men on a good job. No one expected SA'AR to win, but they held their positions long enough for reservists to have relieved them if it had been real war. For the GOLANI Brigade, the exercise's review is conducted in an amphitheater of M113s, and the commanders have nothing but praise for their army of brown berets.

This exercise was a stepping-stone for both infantryman and tanker. They learned from the experience, and will advance to larger scale maneuvers, where they will come to know the true meaning of combined arms and the Ground Corps Command they represent.

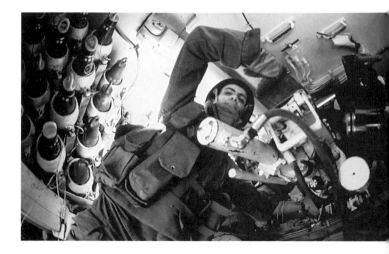

Nomex gloves, cramped conditions, and enough ammo to really cause trouble. An artillery gunner makes final preparations on his "baby."

Soon they'll be off to brigade- and division-sized forays in the vast Negev wasteland, where they'll interact with dozens of other tank units, paratroopers, GIVA'ATI and NA'HA'L infantrymen, combat engineers, artillery batteries, and even attack helicopters and fighter-bombers. Mastering the interservice, interunit interaction will be essential if they are to perform well in future conflicts.

War is a constant threat, and both the GOLANI Brigade and the MERKAVA tankers must return to guard the Golan Heights. But reality will not allow the tankers and infantrymen to maintain an incessant vigil; there are other duties, other places, and different enemies. No matter where these men serve, however, their unit pride dictates a loyalty to the heights, and to its defense. For the GOLANI Brigade, this bond was reinforced by a summer's climb up the peak of Mount Hermon, where the men followed in the bloodied footprints of 1973. By "recapturing" Mount Hermon for a second time, this new generation of GOLANI fighters is remembering the past, so that hopefully it won't be repeated.

Chapter 7
Uprising Duty: NA'HA'L in the Gaza Strip

It was a cold night along Lebanon's border with Israel on 25 November 1987. As the residents of northern Galilee sat in their homes watching television, playing cards, and visiting with neighbors, the northern winds brought something that would forever change their lives. At approximately 2130, Maludin A-naja, a terrorist from the Damascus-based Popular Front for the Liberation of Palestine General Command headed by the notorious Ahmed Jibril, rode with the Levantine winds on a red and white motorized hang glider, crossing high over the Israeli security fence. Although Israeli ground radar detected his aerial foray, he still was able to glide unnoticed on his nylon wings into Israel. Armed with an AKMS, dozens of grenades, a silenced Tokarov pistol, and suicidal determination, this Palestinian "Rambo" could not have realized that his kamikaze efforts that chilly night would forever alter the course of Middle East history.

Landing his hang glider, Maludin headed toward the camp at Beit Hillel. Moving undetected along the northern Galilee hills toward the base, Maludin noticed a white army Peugeot tender on the adjacent road. Placing his AKMS assault rifle on full-auto, Maludin crouched, aimed, and fired a full thirty-round magazine at the vehicle, killing its driver and seriously wounding a female soldier passenger. The sound of gunfire should have sparked a decisive response from

Prior to setting out for a few days of fun and sun in the guise of brigade exercises, NA'HA'L infantrymen listen to the brigade OC give yet another "this is what we are trained for" speech!

Portrait of a much weathered NA'HA'L infantryman.

Observation, detection, and determined firepower: the keys to securing Israel's border with Lebanon. Near Mt. Dov, a heavily armed NA'HA'L M113 patrols the fence.

the nearby base, home of a NA'HA'L infantry battalion, but it didn't. Although intelligence had ordered an alert for the entire north, which should have been intensified by the radar sighting of the hang glider, security at the base was lax. Soldiers sat in their tents reading, relaxing, and playing backgammon with a fervor that should have been directed toward their camp's defense. This gave Maludin his golden opportunity. As he appeared at the base perimeter firing and throwing grenades, the lone and frightened guard at the gate ran from his post without even firing a shot in warning or in anger. The consequences were

immediate. Maludin entered the base and succeeded in killing five NA'HA'L infantrymen and wounding dozens more before a seriously wounded Sgt. Gideon Bashari managed to aim through the sights of his GLILON and lay a burst of 5.56mm fire into Maludin's chest, killing the lone terrorist intruder.

The "Night of the Hang Glider," as it became known in Israeli history, was a mortal blow for the farmer fighters of the NA'HA'L infantry brigade. David Ben-Gurion, modern Israel's patriarch, had long dreamed of an army of farmers, supremely dedicated Zionists who would work the land carrying rifles on their backs. When war would erupt, they would leave their crops and rush to battle, while the hoped-for peace would allow them to "beat their swords into ploughshares." In the midst of the fighting in the summer of 1948, Ben-Gurion's dream was realized with the creation of the NA'HA'L, an acronym for NO'AR HALUTZI LOHEM or "Fighting Pioneer Youth." Originally formed as an extension to the GAD'NA or "Youth Battalions" made up of fifteen to eighteen year olds, NA'HA'L was originally a movement, a trailblazing successor to the first pioneers who turned Palestine's deserts green in the 1920s, to the Tower and Stockade settlements of the 1930s, and to the elite underground PAL'MACH strike force of the 1940s.

By incorporating the Zionist ethic into a military force, the NA'HA'L soldiers attracted the most dedicated, most able-minded and able-bodied of Israel's conscriptable men. Israel's most famous soldiers, such as the mythlike scout Meir Har-Zion, and former Chief of Staff Motta Gur, were all NA'HA'L veterans. In fact, the NA'HA'L's paratroop battalion, the "elite 50th," is one of the IDF's premier combat units. The true NA'HA'L strengths lie in the two fundamentals of their movement: the GAR'IN, or "nuclei from youth groups," who collectively join the IDF after a stint on a kibbutz; and the HE'AHZUT or "outpost settlement." There are two types of outpost settlements in the NA'HA'L vocabulary: One is established at a sensitive border point with the intention of turning it into a *permanent* civilian settlement once a peaceful military situation can be found. The second and perhaps most typical NA'HA'L settlement is one hastily set up along some hot border zone, even though it is not an ideal economical or agricultural location. Life at the HE'AHZUT is usually marked by hard physical toil and exhausting patrols and ambushes. It isn't too horrible, however, considering that each settlement has its share of NA'HA'L female soldiers — Middle Eastern beauties with a pioneering spirit, who just happen to wield a mean UZI!

NA'HA'L's battlefield exploits have been numerous and heroic. During the 1967 Six Day War, NA'HA'L units fought on all three fronts. In the Sinai, the 50th Battalion fought with Col. "Raful" Eitan's 35th Paratroop Brigade along the Rafah-El Arish-Firdan Bridge axis, while NA'HA'L infantry forces took the Egyptian fortress at Um Katef in fierce fighting. Against the Jordanians, NA'HA'L units were active in Latrun and Nablus, while they also participated in the capture of the Golan Heights from Syria. During the War of Attrition, the NA'HA'L border settlements came into their own, serving as vital defensive posts on the new and difficult-to-defend frontiers along the Golan Heights, Jordan Valley, and Suez Canal. During the 1973 Yom Kippur War, the 50th Paratroop Battalion fought a fierce defense of the southern Golan Heights, losing twenty-two killed and hundreds wounded in but a few days of combat. They were then sent into the Sinai, to counterattack against the Egyptian onslaught. Other NA'HA'L units made heroic stands in their suicidal defenses on the Bar-Lev Line fortifications, especially the protracted stand against overwhelming Egyptian forces. When the IDF invaded Lebanon in 1982, NA'HA'L had an untarnished combat record. Its proud history and pioneering ethic made it something of a national institution, and on Independence Day 1982, eleven new NA'HA'L outposts were established. Lebanon, however, would soon prove to be a most difficult war for the farmer soldiers.

Initially, the war went well for the NA'HA'L forces fighting in the Lebanon quagmire. Its units fought in all theaters of combat, proving their worth against Syrian and fanatic Palestinian defenders at Ba'abda, and leftist Muslim Nasserite *Mourabitoun* militia in the approaches to Beirut. Yet all wasn't well in the NA'HA'L camp. NA'HA'L forces suffered a disproportionate number of casualties (sixty-five killed during the first three months of fighting!), and worse, three

A crucial aspect of the NA'HA'L HE'AHZUT or "outpost settlement" is providing security along sensitive borders such as this one in the Jordan Valley.

Israel's neighbors have proved willing to use chemical agents, so gas masks have become a staple issue among all IDF front-line combat units.

NA'HA'L infantrymen were captured by Palestinian gunmen, when they were caught off guard after a "heavy night of backgammon"! They were later exchanged for more than a *thousand* convicted Palestinian terrorists in Israeli jails. The controversial swap dragged the NA'HA'L reputation to an all-time low, and many senior IDF officers, including the chief of staff, reconsidered the military necessity of such a unit. Just when it appeared that the new generation of NA'HA'L soldier farmers would erase the negative image, the "Night of the Hang Glider" transpired. NA'HA'L soldiers were labeled a "national embarrassment," and a public outcry led to charges against some of the officers and conscripts whose lack of discipline had made the terrorist attack possible. Many NA'HA'L soldiers even went so far as to invert the unit tags on their uniforms in shame.

Yet no matter how low NA'HA'L morale had sunk,

it proved to be insignificant compared to what that night would soon produce. If the "Night of the Hang Glider" was a serious mark against the IDF, it was a call to arms for the Palestinians living on the West Bank and Gaza Strip. The killing of six NA'HA'L infantrymen made the once-mighty Israeli soldier a tangible target — the shield of invincibility had eroded. The rage, bitterness, and frustration felt by the inhabitants of the territories were unleashed in a burst of fury. Only a week or so following Maludin's entrance into Palestinian martyrdom, law and order in the territories began to disappear. The most violent rioting would take place in Gaza, and NA'HA'L infantrymen were some of the first soldiers on the scene.

The ancient Philistine port city of Gaza is the picture of squalor. Painfully neglected by the Ottoman Turks, its beachfront area had always been one of the poorest in the Middle East. Fortunes didn't change in 1949, when the Egyptians took over the Gaza Strip and its hundreds of thousands of Palestinian refugees who had fled the fighting of that first Arab-Israeli war. The Egyptians occupied the Gaza Strip with an iron fist, turning it into an army camp, from which they could use Palestinian guerrillas or *fedayeen* to stage terrorist attacks against nearby Israeli settlements. Israel responded with retaliatory air and commando strikes, which only increased the suffering of the local Gazans. Egypt tried to rally the hopes of the refugees by enlisting volunteers for the *fedayeen* raids, promising that one day all of Palestine would be theirs. These dreams were dashed in June 1967, when Israeli paratroopers, led by the NA'HA'L's 50th Battalion, took the city, and much of the Middle East.

For the Palestinians of Gaza, the Israeli occupation was both a blessing and a curse. Living conditions were markedly better, but to many the fact that the ''Zionist'' Army controlled Gaza meant that they would never realize a Palestinian homeland. Soon frustration gave way to rage, and with the advent of a growing Palestinian terrorist movement on the West Bank, in Jordan, and in Lebanon, Gaza became a battleground. Thousands of weapons left behind by the Egyptian Army were now made available to the numerous terrorist cells, allied to Palestinian terror groups, which declared war on the IDF. It was a brutal fight, waged in the streets, the *casbah,* and the olive groves. With law and order lost, the OC of Southern Command, Maj. Gen. Arik Sharon, initiated a fierce counterinsurgency campaign. Using a brilliant intelligence network, and the IDF's most elite units led by Arabic-speaking guides, commandos dressed in civilian garb selectively eliminated the terrorist cell leaders. Trees were cut to diminish guerrilla sniper positions, and hundreds of caves were sealed shut, locking in for eternity their arms caches and unknowing human guards. It was a twenty-four-hour-a-day campaign of blood and fire. It was also a brilliant success. In 1971, there was only a single reported terrorist incident, compared with seven hundred in

1970. Peace, for the next seventeen years, would come to the Gaza Strip. Thousands of the city's men journeyed daily into Israel for jobs, families were built, businesses established, and lives lived. The rage of Palestinian frustration would fester, however, only to be unleashed in the winter of 1987.

Only a week or so after the ''Night of the Hang Glider,'' the troubles began, when false rumors were circulated that Israeli soldiers had intentionally run down Arab workers. At first, the rioting in Gaza began as most instances of public disorder have always begun in the territories — rocks thrown at police and soldiers, burning tires, and a general public strike. Yet something here was markedly different. Thousands of teenagers were in the streets, calls for a *jihad* or holy war were emanating from the mosques, and hundreds of outlawed PLO flags and portraits of a smiling Yasir Arafat began to appear pasted on the walls of many homes of the strip's 650,000 inhabitants. Initially, the Defense Ministry viewed this letting off of steam as nothing out of the ordinary, and dispatched only a small number of army units garrisoned in the town to quell the disturbances. These beleaguered soldiers, having been issued no riot-control gear and with no riot-control training, were under strict orders not to fire unless faced with a life-threatening situation. They found themselves hopelessly outnumbered. The IDF's inability to cope with the Gaza troubles soon led to rioting in the more moderate West Bank; Ramallah, Nablus, and Hebron were turned into battlefields. Molotov cocktails began to appear, followed by a rubber and lead bullet response by the Israeli forces. A new element was introduced when members of the world media converged on the territories in massive numbers. Cameras competed for that perfect shot of brutality, which would substitute ratings for fact, glitz for reality. For Israel, it became a public relations nightmare; for the Israeli soldier, a frustrating war of nerves.

It became known as the *intifadah,* an Arabic word meaning ''uprising,'' although many of its hard-core

مطعم الشرق
سالة

Standing close to an anti-riot mechanized monstrosity that fires marbles, rubber bullets, and real bullets, a NA'HA'L infantryman prepares to lead a patrol through the Jabalia refugee camp.

leaders called it the *intiwadah* or "chaotic state of anarchy." Whatever it was called, it was a civil war, and the IDF found itself with a serious security problem. A battalion of mechanized NA'HA'L infantrymen, ill-equipped and untrained for the task, was rushed into the territories, the eye of the storm. They had just come back from a stint inside the Lebanon security zone, where a few months of battling Shiite suicide bombers and Palestinian infiltrators had taken its toll. They now found themselves in a similar combat situation, only this time Czechoslovakian high explosives were replaced by kitchen-made Molotov cocktails, Soviet-produced hand grenades by slingshots. And

Standing close to an anti-riot mechanized monstrosity that fires marbles, rubber bullets, and real bullets, a NA'HA'L infantryman prepares to lead a patrol through the Jabalia refugee camp.

the openness of Israeli society allowed their every action to be scrutinized by the world on nightly network news.

Day after day, as the rage of the *intifadah* swelled, the overwhelming task of neutralizing it was magnified. One of the principal objectives for the conscript soldiers grunting through the squalor of Gaza was the restoration of order. The IDF General Staff, however, gave conflicting orders to the field. At first, soldiers were told to *not* use excessive force. This was a most difficult order for the eighteen and nineteen year olds to carry out while being showered by rocks, insults, and curses. Another tactic was firing tear gas, though this failed when the young Palestinians learned that sniffing onions could diminish the effects of CS-5, and the protesters became experts at turning the tables on the IDF and throwing back the smoking canisters. When situations got out of hand and lives were threatened, real firepower was employed. In the first 100 days of the *intifadah,* about 100 Palestinians were killed on the West Bank and Gaza. Israel received world scorn for its "inhumane actions," even though only a few months earlier the Egyptians had killed twenty-three Palestinians in Rafah (Gaza's sister city which was split in half by the Camp David Peace Treaty), and in 1982 in a day the Syrians killed 30,000 of their own in the town of Hama — all to the silence of an ambivalent world.

The *intifadah* presented a new challenge to the IDF General Staff. Expert in managing conventional warfare as well as spectacular special forces operations, it now found itself battling an enemy it could not defeat with armor divisions and paratroop commando raids. At first, the order not to use deadly force was issued. Then the situation became intolerable, and the shoot-to-kill order was given. Since it met with such vehement world opposition, however, the General Staff ordered its soldiers in the field to utilize a controversial policy that had worked so brilliantly for the Turks, British, and Egyptians in Gaza: "Break their bones!" Israeli soldiers began to carry batons in order to implement this modern-day "eye-for-an-eye" strategy. Since not one Israeli soldier was ever given riot-control training during his TIRO-NUT, the on-the-job experience amid the *intifadah* led to obvious irregularities and abuses. Unleashing inexperienced and frightened conscripts into the fray did reinstate some semblance of order and respect, but it had its price. Many senior commanders were con-

A NA'HA'L two-man patrol enforces an *intifadah*-inspired curfew. Note the riot control Plexiglas visors on their helmets.

cerned that using combat troops for riot control might have deep implications in the long-held holy "purity of arms" ethic, which dictates the IDF's use of deadly force. From sticks to stones, the IDF tried everything in its resources to quell the *intifadah* without killing unnecessarily, including the mechanical oddity of an armored vehicle set up for firing rubber bullets from ten mounted GALIL assault rifles, and also for firing marbles.

It is April, and for this mechanized NA'HA'L platoon, whose designation will have to remain anonymous, it is the second time in six months they've played "hardball" in the strip. They were first rushed into the *intifadah* in December, when the bone-chilling winter rains were the only relief in sight from the Molotov cocktails, rocks, and tear gas. The soldiers all look a good five years older than they really are — they smoke too much, are too cynical, and look stressed and anxious. Politically the platoon is diverse: Some would throw the Palestinians across the River

Jordan into the Hashemite Kingdom; others firmly believe in giving the Palestinians a state of their own. Views and belief aside, the members of this NA'HA'L platoon realize that they are in the midst of a full-scale war. This is perhaps best understood by Sergeant Herzel from Tel Aviv. Known as "platoon spokesman" for his uncanny ability to have himself filmed by Western newsmen, Sergeant Herzel says: "Sure my enemy might only be thirteen years old, and throwing a stone, but stones, petrol bombs, and dastardly homemade devices of death can kill. The first time I was here, I was almost stabbed to death by the sharpened claws of a garden rake turned into a pair of brass knuckles, were it not for my flak vest and the good lord above. The only difference between a bayonet and a rake is the hate to kill, and here they hate us. Hate is war, and we are in it here up to our asses!"

The platoon is in Gaza now as reinforcements for a GIVA'ATI unit that needed help in the wake of the rioting following the assassination of PLO "number two" man Abu-Jihad in Tunis on April 16, 1988. It

NA'HA'L public relations! A paratroop patrol asks permission of a Gazan senior citizen to search her courtyard for a suspected Molotov cocktail thrower.

is much warmer in Gaza now, compared to the freezing temperatures endured in December, but not much prettier. The sunlight allows one to get a closer look at the squalor and misery and almost makes one understand the fury displayed by the *shahab*, Arabic for "mob," and the basis of the *Shabiba*, the name of an *el-Fatah* youth group known for its cruel treatment of elders not supporting the PLO line. Although the PLO's leadership would have the world believing otherwise, it is the teenagers and smaller children of the *shahab* who have controlled the *intifadah* since the outset. They wear the uniforms of an army — sneakers, dark track suit, and the *kefiyah* headgear. The *kefiyah,* made famous by Yasir Arafat, is as much a symbol of allegiance as is the GOLANI Brigade's brown beret, GIVA'ATI's purple, and the paratroop's red. A red *kefiyah* indicates allegiance to Yasir Arafat, black shows support for a host of Palestinian terror groups based in Syria, and the very few blue *kefiyah*s indicate a pro-Jordanian stance. Yet in Gaza, the color that strikes the greatest fear in the hearts of Israeli soldiers is green, the color of Islam, and the color of the *kefiyah* worn by fanatic Islamic fundamentalists.

Almost every morning, the members of this NA-'HA'L platoon meet the *shahab* face to face, although their twelve-hour patrol begins at midnight. Since Gaza and its surrounding refugee camps are all under curfew, a relative and much-welcomed calm exists in the strip at night, especially in the platoon's patrol sector — the crossroad between Gaza and the Jabalia refugee camp. To keep the rioters in the camp, the IDF has sealed it off with large oil-drum walls, eight feet high, passable only through a thin opening manned twenty-four hours a day by a squad of soldiers. Night patrol is the easiest, since there are no journalists, no instigations, and little rioting. The only activity is the roundup of a known terrorist or riot instigator. A squad surrounds a house while another searches the premises; a third will whisk the suspect into detention. It is nasty work, and makes the residents resent the IDF almost as much as the Israeli soldiers resent

After completing a grueling 30-kilometer forced march toward an "enemy target," squad members share a much-deserved moment of rest.

being there; but as all soldiers have done throughout history, the NA'HA'L infantrymen do what they are told.

Tonight a chilly April quiet has descended over Jabalia, and a roundup is ordered of a man suspected of being a local PLO leader who ordered the fire-bombing of a civilian bus. Just as in Lebanon, night operations are attended to with dire seriousness. The platoon undergoes a lengthy briefing and an even longer weapons check, then proceeds to the target home on foot. Many times during such operations, grenades, sniper shots, or buckets of flaming grease are thrown at the soldiers, and every step is taken with a 360-degree look around. While one squad surrounds the target, insuring no interference from neighbors, the assault team knocks on the door; the door is opened, a quick search is conducted, and the suspect is identified by the accompanying SHIN BET (Israeli

General Security Services) agent. This is the most hated task of all those that the young conscripts must perform. They see themselves as defenders of the state, guardians along the frontiers, not internal security agents knocking on doors in the middle of the night. They nevertheless realize that they may have prevented a firebomb that could have killed or maimed their mothers or sisters. After a well-deserved break for a Coke, a chocolate bar, and numerous cigarettes, the soldiers try to shrug off what they took part in, realizing that the Arab-Israeli conflict knows no boundaries, and knows no rules of engagement.

Night soon blends into morning and morning brings action. After watching the thousands of Gazan males trek off to Israel for their day work at 0300, the NA'HA'L soldiers continue their foot patrols, awaiting the dawn of a new day and the *intifadah*. Lieutenant Ariel is a tall officer with bright red hair covered partially by his black beret. He always commands each patrol a good five steps ahead of his men, and seeming to have eyes in the back of his head, knows exactly where each of his soldiers is positioned. Clutching his CAR-15 with his right hand, Lieutenant Ariel has only to hold out his left hand for his radioman, a new immigrant from Argentina named Michel, to hand him the squad's AN/PRC-77 handset. After checking back with Company HQ, Lieutenant Ariel leads his men deeper into the Jabalia camp. Every fifteen minutes, the mobile element of the patrol rendezvouses with Lieutenant Ariel's men. The three khaki command cars have been fitted with steel nets over all openings, to deflect rocks and Molotov cocktails, and bulldozer blades have been attached to sweep aside roadblocks. The convoy is led by a badly battered jeep carrying a captain, who takes a quick look around and reminds Lieutenant Ariel that "anyone caught throwing stones is to visit the hospital emergency room!" Moments later the foot patrol continues, black boots dragging through empty cigarette packets, stones, and despair.

For their patrol, the soldiers are very well equipped. They carry live ammunition just in case any real trouble takes place, and hundreds of rubber bullets and tear gas canisters. They wear regular Kevlar ballistic infantry helmets with Plexiglas protective visors. Inside their web gear they carry their batons and berets side by side — so no stone thrower will forget just who is doing the *intifadah*-busting. Weighed down and overworked, the patrol walks its beat until it encounters some action. At about 0900, with only three hours remaining in their shift, the fun begins. A small cadre of the *shahab* drags a beaten tire into a crossroad and sets it on fire. When the soldiers come to extinguish the choking inferno, the rocks come showering down. Others soon join in, including mothers who hit, bite, and scratch soldiers chasing the children. If a television camera crew happens to be nearby, hundreds of people converge on the scene, and soon a popular uprising is reported to the world. The soldiers don't really care, and try not to harass the journalists; they know by experience that once the cameras stop rolling, the rioting more or less stops as well.

A PLO flag is spotted on a wall, and Lieutenant Ariel dispatches one of his soldiers to take it down. As the eighteen-year-old soldier, laden down with weapon and gear, negotiates the stone wall, a barrage of rocks and potato grenades rains down on him from a nearby alley. A potato grenade is simply a potato with a dozen sharpened nails driven through it. At long range it hurts; at close range it can kill. As half the squad gives chase to the attackers, the other half fires tear gas and rubber bullets at another *shahab* who has appeared and is in a throwing mood. Eventually, a few are caught and roughed up. Luckily, the situation is resolved before live fire has to be used, although a few Palestinians will always remember that it was the NA'HA'L who obliged them with a beating.

The soldiers prefer shooting tear gas, rubber bullets, and even lead to using their fists, batons, and rifle butts. The twenty-yard no man's land that separates *shahab* from soldier is an oasis that keeps the enemy a safe distance away. The close physical contact and the indignity of the situation lead to very serious anxiety-related problems for the soldiers. It is quite difficult for a nineteen-year-old soldier trained to assault fortified enemy positions to have to stand helpless in rubble while teenagers curse his mother and throw stones and gas bombs at him. Yet restraint is the NA'HA'L infantryman's password. Although he will reply in kind with an obscene gesture and a clenched fist, the infantryman will distance his feelings, rage, and anger at the Palestinian rioters, and perform his duty as well as possible. That's how he was trained, and that's how he'll perform. After all, he owes it to his brigade.

Throughout April and most of May 1988, NA'HA'L called Gaza home. Then they were replaced by the reservists, who in turn began their sixty-two days of annual duty amid the *intifadah* of the Gaza Strip. The NA'HA'L soldiers returned to their training routine, and then to the duty for which they feel best suited — protecting the northern border with Lebanon.

At 0400 on the night of June 23, 1988, a NA'HA'L patrol cruising along the security fence with Lebanon near Mount Dov noticed an attempt by Palestinian terrorists to breach the security fence near Kfar Yuval, an agricultural settlement just 200 yards from the border. With their weapons cocked and flares fired, and in full anticipation of the inevitable firefight, the men, led by patrol commander Lt. Gil Keren, jumped off their BATA'SHIT and ran into battle. Lieutenant Keren ordered his men to open fire, and they hit the four-man terrorist squad with everything they had. The terrorists had hidden in the thick underbrush on the Lebanese side of the fence, but they never had a chance. The pitch dark night was illuminated with thunderous bursts of automatic fire as other units joined in the battle, including OC Northern Command Maj. Gen. Yossi Peled, who got in some target practice of his own. Pinned down, and unable to withstand the NA'HA'L pressure much longer, the terrorists reconsidered their fate. After forty-five minutes of concentrated fire, they surrendered.

The four-man terrorist squad had carried a full

An officer and his radioman — an inseparable commodity on any battlefield.

complement of weaponry, including more than twenty kilograms of high explosives, an RPG, an RPK, and four AK-47s with almost a thousand rounds of ammunition. They were dressed in blue work clothes to disguise themselves as field hands in order to gain entrance to a nearby settlement, and had orders to seize dozens of hostages and commit massive destruction. The terrorists' termination was a well-earned and direly needed victory for the NA'HA'L foot soldiers, who only weeks ago were in Gaza. A young Jerusalemite NA'HA'L private proudly said after the battle: "I didn't volunteer into a combat unit in order to get stones thrown at me. This is the real thing — the reason I wear this uniform, carry this weapon, and guard where I stand now!"

With a joyous elation creeping back into the NA'HA'L ranks after a most difficult eight months, the IDF General Staff decided to boost the brigade's morale even further. In July, in celebration of the NA'HA'L's fortieth anniversary, the brigade received its own distinctive light green beret! Although a "beret does not a unit make," it was a fitting symbol of gratitude to one of the oldest and most embattled of all IDF combat units.

Chapter 8
"Follow Me": The Israeli Officer

On a cool Jerusalem night in April 1988, Israel is paying homage to her war dead. Aside a floodlit and somber Wailing Wall, hundreds of government dignitaries, military commanders, and bereaved families sit silently while prayers for the dead are offered. The soldiers chosen to provide security detail and a ceremonious honor guard for this revered national event are all the vanguard of the Israel Defense Forces: officer cadets from BAHAD 1, literally "training base number one," the factory where Israel produces its officers. Throughout the day, the cadets, identifiable by the white loops over their shoulder epaulets and white circles behind their beret badges, have been patrolling the streets of Jerusalem's old city as a deterrent and reactionary security force. While most Israeli soldiers are busy pressing their Class A's for the upcoming ceremonies, the BAHAD 1 cadets are in full battle kit, the clatter from their radios drowning out the call to prayers from the holy city's churches, mosques, and synagogues. As day is transformed into night, the legion of cadets garrison themselves into positions on rooftops nearby, while another group

of cadets in full Class A garb march stoically onto the parade ground. As BAHAD 1's senior master sergeant shouts the rabble into line, weapons are raised, salutes are offered, and the memorial flame is lit. Mourning has begun.

As the ceremony proceeds, and the military rabbi assists the father of a fallen paratrooper in reciting

The naval officer training school's senior master sergeant tends to the "important" task of fixing his future commander's attire.

BAHAD 1 produces officers like Maj. Gen. Ehud Barak — paratroop officer, commando leader involved in Israel's most secretive and spectacular operations, and one of the most decorated Israeli soldiers.

the KADESH, the Jewish prayer for the dead, the officer cadets are engrossed in deep thought. Perhaps it's the sadness of Memorial Day, and perhaps it's a realization of their own precarious mortality. They know only too well that their duty this special evening is no coincidence: If one fact remains constant in the IDF, it is that officers are killed in far greater proportion than all other ranks combined. It is the ultimate price that thousands of Israeli officers have paid in the past forty years of war, and a tradition it seems will continue. For self-sacrifice, leading from the front and by example, is the meaning of command in the IDF.

Amid worshipers, officer candidates maintain a faithful vigil in the Old City of Jerusalem.

Those who have volunteered for the officers' course are the best soldiers found in the IDF, and once they receive their commissions, they're expected to become even better. They'll have to be, for they are to join one of Israel's most exclusive clubs. The IDF's most courageous, celebrated, and capable warriors have all been BAHAD 1 graduates. Soldiers like former Chief of Staff Lt. Gen. "Raful" Eitan, a member of the

PAL'MACH, who although gravely wounded in the 1948 fighting in Jerusalem continued to serve as one of the paratroop's most brilliant, audacious, and innovative commanders. Or Brig. Gen. Avigdor Kahalani, recipient of two bravery medals, and savior of northern Israel in 1973 as commander of the elite 7th Armored Brigade's 77th Battalion fighting in the "Valley of Tears."

While these brilliant commanders have succeeded in cheating death, too many Israeli officers haven't. Men like Maj. Guni Harnik, a commander of the GOLANI Brigade's elite reconnaissance battalion, who after being discharged from active service just days prior to the 1982 invasion of Lebanon, returned to his unit to lead *his* men on the assault on Beaufort Castle. Harnik had trained for years to capture this old crusader's castle from the PLO, and not being at the helm of the assault was for him a sacrilege. Willing to sacrifice his civilian life for his battalion, Major Harnik sacrificed even more when a Palestinian gunner's RPK burst ended his life. Yet perhaps Israel's most famous soldier was Lt. Col. "Yoni" Netanyahu. Serving in the paratroopers and other more secretive elite units, Yoni earned the reputation of a supreme leader. He would reach the history books the way a majority of Israeli officers do, posthumously, as he was killed leading the rescue force at Entebbe in July 1976.

The combat officer has developed into a national institution. Their actions, heroics, and cool leadership under the greatest adversities have been *the* decisive factor leading to Israel's victories in all its wars. Yet how the IDF chooses its officers is just as important as their performance in combat. In the IDF, rank is not a privilege belonging to the right class, but a right of one's self worth. In Syria, for example, only Alawite Muslims, and those faithful to the official government party line, can become commissioned officers, whereas in Jordan, it sure helps to be Bedouin and loyal to King Hussein. In the IDF, however, it doesn't matter whom you voted for, what your social

Awaiting their turn in the Memorial Day ceremonies, naval officer cadets nervously assemble in their dress whites.

standing is, or where your parents came from. All that matters is that you are among the best in your unit, and each soldier is judged from day one of his military service.

All future IDF officers, with the exception of pilots and naval ship commanders, begin their three years of military duty as lowly privates. After a three- to five-month basic training stint in their respective corps, they are posted to their designated units to endure the trials and tribulations of IDF operational service. Through their performance in advanced unit training and in operational forays, their skills and qualities as leaders are examined and noted by their NCOs and officers. After five months of intensive scrutiny, each soldier is judged on his KABA or "quality indicator" (a point system that grades all of the soldiers' personal characteristics, background, and potential) and by his commander's own evaluation. If

111

the marks are right, he is sent to a squad leader's course for the rank of sergeant, or as it's known in the IDF, KOURS MAK'IM.

The squad leaders' courses, be they for tankers, paratroops, or combat engineers, are considered the most arduous of all. Most of this grinding learning experience takes place in the field, with incessant assault and weapons drills, navigation instruction, and of course, the beloved IDF forced marches. Yet beyond the sweat and aching muscles, squad leader candidates learn the most important lesson — basic leadership qualities. As the commander of a squad of future combat engineer squad leaders, First Ser-

geant Tal says: "In basic training, the soldiers were taught their 'combat ABCs,' but here they're going to have to learn how to produce words and sentences with their new-found knowledge. Instead of participating in a mock assault as riflemen, they'll be ordered to 'instinctively' come up with the proper tactics as commanders." It isn't a natural process, and will take about twenty hours a day for the next three months to accomplish.

Memorial Day in Israel: With the remnants of the Jewish temple as a backdrop, the flag is lowered to half mast, weapons raised, and the honorary flame ignited.

Although squad leader's course is the first rung in the ladder of command, its successful completion does not guarantee anything. The newly commissioned sergeant is reassigned to his old unit, where he will serve as a squad or team leader, or as a tank or artillery gun commander. He can then count on a further six to ten months of operational duty, training, and the other day-to-day joys of being an Israeli soldier. This is the period when the NCO displays his practical military leadership, be it directing an ambush inside Lebanon, securing a section along the Jordanian-Israeli border, or helping out a soldier with a personal problem.

Officer training is more than ceremonies and parades: it is learning the techniques of command from the battlefield masters. Here a senior paratroop officer shares his knowledge.

With approximately one year remaining in the soldier's mandatory three of national service, his review for officer's course comes up. Only those with the highest KABA scores are even considered, and this is followed by additional means of selection, including peer reviews, recommendations by commanding officers, and psychological evaluations. Positive traits for acceptance into officer's course are: *sociability;*

social intelligence; emotional stability; leadership capabilities; devotion to one's unit; and *duty, decisiveness, innovation,* and most importantly, *perseverance under stress and fire.* A soldier who cannot handle himself under fire will not be able to raise his hand as an officer and shout "follow me!" in combat. This is not something judged on a psychological chart, but observed in the field. By the time most Israeli soldiers reach their twentieth birthday, they have already had their "baptism under fire."

Finally, after two years of training, security duty, more training, squad leader's course, and even more training, the selected NCOs are ushered into BAHAD

1. There are three types of officer's courses available: a six-month paratroop and infantry course; the three-month "basic" course for all noncombatant cadets; and a two-part course for tankers, artillerymen, combat engineers, and air-defense crewmen. The latter is known as the AGA'M, or "operations" course, and is the most distinct of all officer training, since it allows soldiers from different branches of service to

interact and learn different aspects of the IDF's other combat units. So with little fanfare, even less increase in pay, and the promise of physical and mental challenge unequaled in their lives, a few hundred NCOs pass through the gates of BAHAD 1. Their lives will be forever changed.

BAHAD 1 has been described as brutally intensive, harsh, and unrelenting; it is "affectionately" called the IDF's "pressure cooker." If basic training is remembered by its "us against them" view of command, and squad leader's course is too hurried for any thought whatsoever, then officer's course is best characterized by the dignity the instructors offer their cadets. They are treated like officers, and as a result are expected to behave as such. They are not punished for minor infractions or expected to conform to rigid military discipline. They are in BAHAD 1 because they want to be, and because they are a cut above everyone else. They have all dreamed of that still-distant ceremony in which they'll receive their commissions, yet the day when they'll be able to take a salute instead of giving one is still but a fantasy. The attrition rate at BAHAD 1 is about 50 percent, a generous margin when considering that the pilot's course drops more than 90 percent of all its candidates!

The IDF takes great pride in the heritage of its officers and the history of BAHAD 1. Senior commanders remember when the IDF didn't have the luxury of training its officers in such a perfect time-tested facility. During the days of the pre-independence HAGANAH (Hebrew for "defense"), commanders were chosen for their physical and mental stamina, and not much more, as not much more was available. As an illegal and poorly funded movement, the HAGANAH could field very few weapons and support very few units. As a result, commanders were forced to draw from the only resources in abundant supply — their imaginations, and innovative responses to military predicaments. Innovation soon became a contagious commodity in the HAGANAH, and commanders, unable to draw upon a long heritage of military strate-

gies, soon developed hard-hitting tactics and leadership ethics of their own. Since few guns and trained men were on hand for HAGANAH operations, commanders were forced to lead from the front in order to insure that their meager resources were used to maximum potential.

When the elite PAL'MACH strike companies were formed with British blessings during the darkest hours of World War II, the HAGANAH soon understood what a potent combination decisive command and firepower made. Yet the most important aspect of the PAL'MACH became producing commanders who were egalitarian, accessible, and, most of all, who led men by example, not from the rear. Discipline was never rigid, few salutes were offered, and the men considered their officers as friends rather than distant symbols of authority. In fact, few distinctions between commander and common soldier existed in pay, living conditions, and privileges, except of course when the officer clutched his Sten submachine gun, raised his hand, and shouted "follow me!"

In the 1948 War of Independence, the newly formed IDF officers' corps inherited the PAL'MACH command ethic. This led to military victory after victory. A distinctive officer mentality began to evolve — a determination to have their own way. Stubbornness became a call sign for officers and NCOs alike. BAHAD 1's commander is a good example. An innovative and war-tested commander, Colonel Moti realizes that the discipline of command is what brought him through service in the paratroops, first as a simple rifleman, later as a paratroop battalion commander during the 1982 invasion of Lebanon, and as sector commander along the Lebanese border during the height of terrorist activity. Yet in fitting with the independent bent of most IDF officers, Colonel Moti had not only stubbornly refused his initial call-up to officer's course, but had disobeyed orders to "volunteer" into the course until he received a written guarantee that he'd be returned to his paratroop reconnaissance unit upon graduation. He now commands the training and discipline of thousands of future stubborn officers, who also will refute and question orders when they see fit. Proudly, however, Colonel Moti states that BAHAD 1 today produces the best officers in IDF history.

Immediately following the traumatic Lebanon War, a serious malaise overtook the IDF psyche. No one saw this more clearly than the junior officers just graduated from BAHAD 1. When these newly commissioned second lieutenants returned to their paratroop platoons, tank forces, and artillery batteries, they found the simple soldier indifferent and anxious. Leading through example, the hallmark of all IDF traditions, made little impact when soldiers did not care about their orders and assignments. This sad period in IDF history became known as ROSH KATAN or "small head," a reference to the know-nothing, see-nothing, do-nothing attitude of soldiering. Motivation in the IDF was eventually reinstated by a fiercely patriotic and zealous junior officer corps — twenty-year-old men who, after spending but a few months in BAHAD 1, were able to arouse their soldiers. These green officers led by example, sacrificing their personal comforts and leaves for the men in their care, and succeeded in restoring morale to a demoralized army.

So how does BAHAD 1 produce such fine officers? The daily routine of the cadets is long, with little respite for relaxation or even study time. Wake-up is at 0500, followed by a daily itinerary that includes an array of inspections, combat training, classes in military theory, communications, tactics, logistics, navigation, and IDF history, then intensive night-time combat training. It should be noted that BAHAD 1 is set up like any combat-ready base, with its complement of cadets organized into battalions, companies, platoons, and squads. In early April 1988, this course was dispatched to serve alongside conscript GOLANI, GIVA'ATI, and paratroop units on the Lebanese border during a period of heightened Palestinian terrorist activity. The stress of duty along the Lebanese border was exacerbated by the fact that the cadets were all

under intense pressure to perform as platoon leaders. After all, the BAHAD 1 motto is inscribed in each soldier's mind: "You will be treated as officers until your actions warrant otherwise."

At the onset of the course, "future officers acting like privates" seems odd, inconsistent, and clumsy. Yet it has its purpose, and after a few weeks, unit cohesion, and the cohesive nature of command, begins to make its appearance. In the field, the competitiveness that raised its head during the initial phase of classroom study at BAHAD 1 evaporates into a "one for all and all for one" camaraderie. For the duration of the course, each soldier will alternate on a PA'KA'L or "infantry support weapon's role." In basic they might have been a MAG gunner or carried an RPG, but here they will have the opportunity to experiment and learn the tactical deployment of each infantry support weapon in the IDF inventory. Although these cadets aren't infantrymen, they *must* master everything associated with small-scale combat scenarios. In order to lead by example, they must know more than the men they'll command in the field. As Lieutenant Colonel D., deputy base commander, told the cadets after MAG firing exercise followed by a particularly grueling forty-kilometer forced march: "Every IDF officer must know how to fight in an open field and amid urban ruin. Every IDF officer must know how to direct his men in battle, and when to order them to open fire. Most importantly, every IDF officer must master the art of infantry warfare, even if he'll be directing combat one day from the confines of a MERKAVA tank!"

The curriculum at BAHAD 1 is as intense as it is varied. The future officers learn almost everything conceivable, from the Bar-Kochba and his rebellion against Rome, to sociopolitical development of Israeli economics, to the names of birds inhabiting the Negev Desert. Mostly, however, they study war — something Israel has had its share of! In one of the classrooms, a large map of the state of Israel and the Middle East has been marked off with red circles showing exactly where major battles have been fought. There are so many battlefields, that the circles almost cover the map. Some marks are as close to home as Jerusalem, some as distant as Beirut, Damascus, and Tunis; there is even a pointer in Entebbe's direction. Other marks will be added in the years to come.

Today's history lesson concentrates on the brutal 1967 to 1970 War of Attrition, and in particular, the 9 September 1969 commando raid against Egyptian lines, code-named "Operation RAVIV." To achieve maximum surprise, IDF paratroop and tank units deployed from captured Egyptian vehicles still with their original markings. For more than twenty-four hours, the ex-Egyptian T-54s and BTR personnel carriers caused havoc behind enemy lines. The professor this afternoon is an always-smiling reservist officer whom the cadets have seen dozens of times on the base, not realizing that as a second lieutenant during Operation RAVIV, he had commanded a tank section that destroyed an entire Egyptian munitions dump. The two-hour lecture does not concentrate on deployment, logistics, or history, but on the meaning of the operation to a junior officer. By examining the

Amidst the yellow cloud of a simulated gas attack, officer cadets endure the strain of a forced stretcher march, in full NBC gear.

difficulties, dilemmas, and objectives that the former second lieutenant faced years back, when as a recent BAHAD 1 graduate he had commanded soldiers in a difficult and innovative operation, the cadets are given brain "fodder" for use in the inevitable combat scenarios in their future.

Israel's overabundance of a combat heritage, and a wealth of commanding officers who have been in the thick of it, allows the cadets to learn the "follow-me" theory of command firsthand. Since each cadet has already experienced two years of service, and courses in a combat unit, the emphasis on academics is minimal. Instead, the instructors concentrate on developing the future officer's ability to solve tactical and human problems, as well as the necessary leadership skills needed to implement these solutions.

Perhaps one of the greatest tests of this "method training" was in sending the cadets to the West Bank city of Hebron in month number five of the *intifadah*. Hebron, a holy city to both Muslim and Jew and a constant hotbed of Palestinian nationalism, was the scene of some of the *intifadah*'s worst rioting. Sent into the labyrinth of rocks, Molotov cocktails, and frustration, the officer cadets found themselves behaving in a totally different manner than they had months earlier as corporals and sergeants. They had learned to act in a more decisive and innovative way. Instead of *reacting* to incidents, they now used their new-found skills to gain the upper hand over the *shahab*. With a minimum of violence, the BAHAD 1 platoons, adorned with their white tape ranks, were able to restore peace and normality to an abnormal situation. Officer cadet Ronen, an SP-109 155mm self-propelled gun commander who was in Gaza when the *intifadah* erupted in December 1987, commented: "It was frightening, confusing, and frustrating for us on the line. But now, the picture of command is clear in my head, and I now know what my former platoon commander did wrong, and what I'd do in his shoes."

One of the most fascinating aspects of BAHAD 1 is its ability to unify all elements of the IDF into one distinct body. By including cadets from all the different branches of the IDF into one base and platoon, the basic codes of the "Israeli officer" are implanted into each candidate whether he wears a black, gray, or blue beret. Among the cadets, a fantastic esprit de corps can be found. The realization that for one to do well, they all must excel, inspires very definite unit pride, and prejudices are overlooked. Sure the combat engineers enjoy saying that "all tankers are like a piece of ripe meat, waiting to be burned to a delicate medium rare," and tankers like to joke that "all artillerymen are deaf . . . what did you say?" The artillerymen like to call the Air Defense cadets "pigeon assassins," and everyone sounds the cadence of combat engineers marching — "left . . . left . . . left . . . left," a cruel reference to the frequency with which combat engineers lose legs while searching for mines. Yet the jokes relieve the extreme tension of the course. Second Platoon has already seen ten of its own thrown out, and the laughter helps them in their unified attempt to pass the course and become officers.

Two months into the course, and these cadets are already different soldiers than they were when they walked through the gates eight weeks ago. Burned into each cadet's memory is the first day at BAHAD 1: receiving the white tape rank insignia, meeting the squad commander, and most importantly, having the initial interview with the platoon commander (who is either a captain, major, or lieutenant colonel). Contact with the commanding officer, and a senior one no less, is a crucial aspect in the long haul that transforms sergeants into lieutenants. The CO's accessibility, and his ability to have an open and frank relationship with his men, makes the BAHAD 1 nickname of "officer factory" a misnomer. The cadets need this kind of support, for the pressure at BAHAD 1 intensifies as the course goes on. The psychological pressure of being under constant scrutiny begins to take its toll. The cadets become sensitive to the smallest details of their behavior, dress, and performance. The most minute and insignificant mistake might be the determining factor in their being returned to their old unit as a failure.

Officer cadet Beni was one of 2d Platoon's best candidates. Always willing to help his friends, he excelled in his studies, and in the field was second to none. Yet even though he could field strip a .50-caliber machine gun in seconds, master the ins and outs of the AN/PRC-77 field radio, and navigate his way through the most nonnegotiable wadi, the pressure of the course became too heavy a burden. Gathering his dignity, cadet Beni packed his gear and signed a voluntary withdrawal from BAHAD 1, returning to the "relaxed" atmosphere of his beloved 7th Armored Brigade in the very relaxed Golan Heights!

Cadet Beni's story is a typical case. As the base psychologist states: "The cadets come here with bright eyes and wild expectations. They heard from friends and relatives that BAHAD 1 was an 'inhumane assembly line for mass producing officers,' and they soon find it difficult to meet the standards. They were told to just pass by, and at best, remain anonymous with your commander. But it never works, and the pressure gets to everyone."

It is a hazy May morning at 0500, and already the entire battalion of AG'AM cadets have assembled on the parade grounds in neat rows of three. Although there are but two weeks remaining until their graduation, they haven't gathered to practice march and drills. Instead of smartly pressed Class As, they are in full combat gear, each soldier carrying his weapon, pack, and large field map, which can mean only one thing — a navigation exercise! For the next twelve hours they'll negotiate the wilds of central Israel with compass and map in hand. The spring's strong sun has already appeared, and the weight of the web gear, weapon, and the unknown begins to take its toll. The agony and sweat of one more navigation exercise don't matter much, for in two weeks it will all be over. A group photo will be taken, sweatshirts with the course's name and slogan will be made up, and

the sweet smell of command will become a reality. In a charged-up ceremony in front of parents and friends, a high-ranking officer will walk up to each cadet and remove the white tape covering second lieutenant bars aboard the shoulders, and the white tape covering the officer qualification badge on the left collar. This warrants a quick salute, and the new officer will never be the same. His transition from soldier to officer will be a marked one. He'll have high expectations, limitless objectives, and a newfound sense of responsibility for the twenty to forty men in his command. Self-sacrifice sometimes has a permanent price.

On 14 July 1988, Lt. Uri Maoz, a twenty-two-year-old paratroop officer from the brigade's elite reconnaissance battalion SAYERET TZANHANIM, led his platoon in pursuit of *Hizballah* terrorists inside the twelve-mile-wide security zone near the Israeli border inside Lebanon. Hours earlier, the terrorists had fired Katyusha rockets into northern Israel from the village of Ko'echba, and Lieutenant Maoz was determined to hunt them down. In a cactus grove, Lieutenant Maoz's eagle eye discovered three bearded men wearing camouflage fatigues and carrying RPGs. He ordered his men into firing position, and in the brief firefight the three Shiites were martyred. Just as Lieutenant Maoz radioed in to his brigade commander to report the battle, another *Hizballah* squad fired on the paratroopers, and Lieutenant Maoz was killed by RPG fire, the first and only Israeli casualty. He was buried in his hometown, Moshav Yisod Hama'aleh, next to his favorite uncle, Lt. Col. Yoav Vespi, who was killed leading his tank battalion on the Golan Heights in 1973, and next to his cousin, Lieutenant Colonel Vespi's son Dudu, a SAYERET TZANHANIM officer killed near Beirut in 1982. At the funeral, paratroop brigade commander Colonel A. said that the paratroops had lost one of their most promising officers. Yet Israel had lost much more. It lost another one of her sons, a leader who, through excellence, dedication, and determination, had tried to make a difference.

Chapter 9
Young Women and Old Men: Female and Reservist Soldiers

Every night at 9:00 P.M., Israeli families sit down together to watch the evening news. The half-hour broadcast is clearly the most popular television show in all of Israel, but not because of its entertainment value. In fact, most of the news is discouraging and depressing. Yet most Israelis feel a sense of nationalistic responsibility in watching the evening news; after all, anything from a terrorist attack nearby to the threat of Syrian invasion can be reported. Sometimes the news is interrupted by a military message of national importance. With a huge official IDF logo providing background on the video monitor, the anchorman reads the following: "FROM THE IDF'S CHIEF OF STAFF'S OFFICE, ALL SOLDIERS AND OWNERS OF VEHICLES ATTACHED TO THE FOLLOWING UNITS WHOSE CODE NAMES SHALL BE READ NOW, PLEASE HEAD FOR YOUR UNITS IMMEDIATELY!" In Israel, this is the beginning of a national mobilization — for either an exercise or a national emergency.

For the next three or four hours, television and radio reports will repeat a litany of jumbled code words. "WHITE HORSE" . . . I repeat . . . "WHITE HORSE" . . . "MIGHTY SWORD" . . . I repeat . . . "MIGHTY SWORD" . . . "HUNTING DOG" . . . I repeat . . . "HUNTING DOG" . . . etc. The anchorman will repeat a long list of words or phrases, which are meaningless to

Too old to return to their combat units, graying reservists are assigned a simple antiterrorist patrol near the Old City of Jerusalem.

Welcome to the army, girls! After exchanging their makeup for gun grease, designer cloths for khakis, new female soldiers line up for inspection on day one of basic training.

most, but to select and anxious individuals, it's an invitation to change from civilian into soldier. They'll don their wrinkled fatigues, fetch their gear, and kiss their wives and children good-bye before heading into the unknown. They proceed by any means available to assembly points throughout Israel, be they supermarket parking lots or airport tarmacs. If they see a fleet of military trucks and dozens of officers in fatigues and full kit, they'll know that something serious is afoot and they won't be heading home for a while. If they are greeted by familiar faces and smiles, it's just, thank God, another exercise. The support personnel handling this reserve callup are almost entirely women soldiers. Female "warriors," who in their respective armor, infantry, and artillery units serve as secretaries, operators, and clerks, in the event of war are expected to fill the ranks of men called up to combat duty. This combination of old fighting men and young women soldiers is, oddly enough, one of Israel's secret weapons — the muscle behind the IDF's potent punch.

Women have been actively involved in the defense of the Jewish homeland since large-scale Jewish immigration to Palestine began in the late eighteenth century. The early Zionists promoted equality among the sexes, and women settlers soon found themselves as full-fledged combatants in the HASHOMER (the "Guard"), the first organized Jewish fighting force in Palestine. In the struggle for an independent Jewish state, chronic manpower shortages forced women to assume tasks once filled only by men. In the prestate undergrounds such as the IRGUN and "Stern Gang," women served as radio operators, messengers, intelligence officers, and even explosive experts. In the militarily elite PAL'MACH, women were embraced as

Female reservists usually get the lackluster assignments such as this one — body searching Jordanian women crossing into Israel. Although a most unpleasant task, the searches are important for security.

Today you are officers! A graduating class of Adjunctory Corps second lieutenants, including an OLAH or "new immigrant" from Ethiopia, clutch their M-16s and wait for their lieutenant bars.

equals, and excelled in the intense military and weapons training — a fact not lost on the organization's British sponsors, who recruited several of the women to parachute behind Nazi lines in Central Europe. When the fight for Israel's independence reached its turning point in the 1948 War, the dire circumstances pushed many women into combat roles, and hundreds were killed. It was the supreme price to pay for survival, and one the IDF vowed never to pay again.

Following the 1948 War, women were conscripted but never placed in combat units. They were organized under an umbrella command, known by the Hebrew acronym for Women's Corps, CHEN, which is also the Hebrew word for "charm." CHEN limited women in the IDF to support roles, although in wars and security alerts it was difficult to keep Israel's women fighters out of the action. During the 1956 Sinai War, three female Air Force pilots flew C-47s that dropped

124

paratroopers at the Mitla Pass; in 1973, two women officers were decorated for valor for their role in tending to wounded and traumatized soldiers close to the front lines. By 1982, the integration of CHEN within the IDF was complete. In the rear echelon, women soldiers fulfilled all the communications, logistics, and intelligence needs of the troops fighting in Lebanon; women maintained fighter aircraft, analyzed aerial reconnaissance photos, and supervised communications and command and control functions for units in the field. Today, not a single IDF unit could perform its allotted task without the contribution of CHEN.

According to the 1959 Military Service Law, all eighteen-year-old females are conscripted into the IDF for two years of service with the exception of those who are married, have criminal records, or can prove religious convictions. The latter has proven to be most controversial, since most secular Israeli believe that *all* citizens should help carry the burden of national defense. Nevertheless, "conscriptable" women are welcomed into the IDF in much the same way men are. They go through the BA'K'UM maze, undergo a less intense basic training (where if they're lucky they will learn to shoot both the UZI and M-16), and are then dispatched to their respective units. Besides regular IDF units, there are two exclusively female units: The first is YAHAS (the Hebrew word for "rapport"), an auxiliary nursing unit in development border towns; the second is HIBA (the Hebrew acronym for "female soldiers in police service," and also the Hebrew word for "affection"), a parapolice patrol force. Both "girls-only" units draw their ranks from girls from broken homes, with minimal education, and for whom service in the IDF is one of the few

Amid the traffic and chaos of Tel Aviv's Central Bus Station, a HIBA patrol assembles for a mid-afternoon briefing and gossip!

directions into mainstream Israeli society.

HIBA's principal military objective is antiterrorist patrols in city streets, marketplaces, and places of public gathering such as post offices and bus stations. Although HIBA soldiers don't carry weapons or communications devices, they do present a capable deterrent force, which combs the patrolled areas for hidden explosive devices, while also acting as a reactive force, responding to emergencies by assisting police and military forces in evacuating civilians. Twenty-year-old Dorit has been a HIBA soldier for almost two years, and has already begun her countdown for days remaining in uniform. Originally she wasn't supposed to have been conscripted into the IDF at all, especially since her ailing and widowed mother needed her close by. Dorit, however, was adamant about not missing out on the national experience, and forced her way into the IDF. Initially, HIBA offered little to

Two paratroop medics sit atop their ambulance eating ices and reading — a favored IDF form of relaxation.

125

Reservists are rarely placed into rear positions; they train for their only true objective — combat operations. In 1973, reservists saved both the Golan and Sinai fronts.

of thousands of women soldiers serving as clerks and secretaries cannot boast of having an exciting military career, some conscripted women opt for a little more razzle-dazzle. In the IDF today, women can be naval radar operators monitoring developments on the Lebanese coast, parachute jump instructors, medical orderlies, teachers of illiterate and new immigrant soldiers, paratroop assault instructors, weapons experts, HAWK SAM battery operators, maintenance "men" for M113s and SP-109 artillery pieces, and even infantry platoon commanders. Yet it's been their nonconventional role as armor instructors at JULIS, the IDF's Tank School, that has really made the difference in separating "the men from the women."

Women first started teaching the art of tank warfare in 1974. The 1973 War had reduced the Armored Corps to dangerously low levels of men and equipment, so that every available tank and crew was stationed along the very volatile frontiers. With all regular army and reservists stationed at the front, the Armored Corps turned to its only remaining reserve — women. In brilliant fashion, they answered the challenge, and trained thousands of tankers, including the conscripts and reservists who so brilliantly battered Syrian armor in the Beka'a Valley in 1982. First Sergeant Orly is only five feet three inches tall, does not have a driver's license, and has a high, unauthoritative voice. Yet she is an expert in the operations, functions, and maintenance of the M-60 Centurion, and her personal favorite, the MERKAVA. Through her dedication, intelligence, and indisputable ability to command, she has been entrusted to teach a future generation of tank soldiers the A to Zs of what she calls "beautiful" armored fighting vehicles. Whereas male instructors use coercion, threats, and insults to pull their ranks in line, Orly uses the kind of intimida-

Dorit, as it seemed boring, pointless, and beneath her. Serving in Tel Aviv's Central Bus Station, however, allowed Dorit to be close to home, available every afternoon to help her mother. With her IDF-issue pocketbook, police arm band, and a well-experienced eye, Dorit walks in group patrols throughout the bus lanes, and among the hurried passengers and Byzantine-style stalls. In her brief military career, she has developed a keen eye for trouble. Dorit has found one Palestinian bomb — an abandoned suitcase containing a mortar shell attached to a sophisticated timing device — and has helped Border Guard policemen detain a known PLO suspect. Although her service was precarious at best, she and her HIBA comrades *have* made a difference.

While service in YAHAS and HIBA cannot be considered the most glamorous in the world, and the tens

"Slightly balding," a bit overweight, and thinking of an ice-cold beer at the beach — a middle-aged reservist awaits heading out on patrol inside the Lebanese security zone.

No jokes about women drivers at the IDF Tank Corps Training Base —most of the instructors are female. They teach future tank fighters everything from the mechanics of armor warfare to how to handle one of the big boys, a MERKAVA MBT, in battle.

tion only a woman can master. She firmly believes that "one can catch more bees with honey." Orly is quick to add that she's no pushover: "No matter what these guys might think, the fact that I have three hard-earned stripes on my sleeves is the deciding factor that must be taken into consideration. And of course it takes a woman's touch!"

Oddly enough, the close proximity of men and women serving and living together in army bases does not create too many serious infractions of discipline. In fact, the presence of women soldiers adds a touch of gentility at army camps that probably helps keep male Israeli soldiers happy. There is absolutely no separation of the sexes in the mess, canteen, and recreation room. Strict military regulations forbid males soldiers from being near women's quarters, but nothing can keep true love apart! In fact, most Israeli husbands and wives meet, fall in love, and court while serving in the army. The "romancing among the web gear," an inevitable product of service in the IDF, is also a thought in the minds of Israeli wives who send their husbands off to reserve duty!

The fact that the IDF is forced to mobilize its aging reservists is a constant reminder of just how precarious Israel's military situation is. A common Israeli expression on the reality of reserve duty can be loosely translated as follows: "There are no civilians in Israel, just soldiers on leave ten months of the year." Every year, the average Israeli male will spend about sixty-two days in uniform, in places as far off and dangerous as Lebanon, the Golan Heights, and the Gaza Strip. They'll do everything from ambushing a Shiite terrorist convoy, to putting down a Palestinian uprising, to such lackluster work as packing ammunition crates at a base somewhere in central Israel. In fact, the MILUIMNIKIM or "reservists" have become as much a part of the Israeli landscape as the Jerusalem panorama, Metzada, and the Mediterranean coast. At many times, Israel appears to be a sea of olive; all one can see on a city street are uniforms worn by men whose aging figures, sloppy demeanor, and disgusted manner of carrying their M-16s make the nickname "soldiers of necessity" all too accurate.

In the IDF, the notion of mobilizing men until the ripe old age of fifty-five is the slow process of demobilizing a soldier at the end of his three years of national service. When a twenty-one-year-old Israeli soldier heads to BA'K'UM on the final day of his 1,095-day service, he knows his time in the IDF has only just begun. For the next thirty-four years, he'll be receiving his sixty-two-day callup notice in the mail, and his stints may be in rain, sandstorms, or blizzards. If death and taxes are inevitable, so is reserve duty. Historically, the reserves have proven to be the decisive factor in winning Israel's wars. According to IDF strategic planners, conscript units stationed along the frontiers are meant to hold off any enemy invasion for little more than twenty-four hours, which is just enough time to mobilize, equip, and transport the reservists. In 1973, the reservists literally saved Israel from a disastrous defeat. On the Golan Heights, reservist armor brigades made their way to the fighting in just the nick of time to save the front, and much of northern Israel. While in the Sinai front, the reservists reached the desert passes at just the right moment to hold off the Egyptian onslaught, and turned defeat into victory. Traditionally, the reservists have been the best educated, the most sensitive to casualty, and the most cautious Israeli soldiers. They have been called by many senior Israeli commanders "the IDF's sure thing."

Service in the reserve is much like an extended high school reunion. Men who matured together while serving their mandatory three years meet on an annual basis. Backs are slapped, pictures of children are displayed, and the relief of escaping mundane lives of marriage and business is cheerfully discussed by men who seem to enjoy the transition from civilians into soldiers. The reserves are also the most integrated and egalitarian of anything the IDF can offer. Lawyers, professors, nuclear engineers, and millionaire businessmen serve in the same units and under the same conditions as fruit vendors, mechanics, and factory workers. In fact, bosses sometimes reach their reservist duty only to find themselves commanded by their employees! Although the reserves is the ultimate integration of Israeli society, and everyone seems happy to see old familiar faces, it must be remembered that this isn't a vacation. Reservists train in highly realistic and physically trying conditions, and they know that should war erupt, they will be the ones expected to save the day and bring about victory.

Sergeant Uri is a forty-two year old from Haifa, who during his ten months of "leave" is a successful travel agent. As a tank gunner, he has already been in the thick of three major wars: the Sinai in 1967, Damascus in 1973, and Beirut in 1982. He has seen just about as much as he wants of war, blood, and destruction. Yet when his callup comes, he dons his uniform, more out of reflex than desire, and heads

Few women soldiers enjoy being treated like porcelain dolls! These infantry assault instructor trainees take on all the "rough and tumble" IDF training, including forced marches.

out toward his unit — a reserve armor brigade considered one of the finest of all reserve units. Luckily, he won't be sent to the territories this time; the destination is his second home, the Golan Heights. For the next eight weeks or so, he'll train, take in target practice, and be placed on operational alert against any hostile noises originating from the Syrian side of the border. Ironically, Sergeant Uri will undergo advanced medical training during this his twenty-first stint in the reserves, so that in the eventuality of war, he'll be able to treat the wounds he has already seen too many of. His medical instructor is a young girl who could very well be his daughter. With dark curls, an UZI, and an authoritative personality, nineteen-year-old Sergeant Sarah will teach the veteran Sergeant Uri the latest advances in treating horrific burns. And so it goes — a scene that could take place only in the IDF!

Appendix: IDF Weaponry

INFANTRY EQUIPMENT

AK-47   The Soviet AK-47 7.62mm assault rifle (as well as the entire AK family of 7.62mm weapons) has been captured in such large quantities from the Egyptians, Syrians, and Palestinians in the wars since 1967 that it became a standard IDF infantry weapon. It is mainly issued to "elite" units.

AN/PRC-25/77   An American field radio of Vietnam vintage used by practically all IDF units.

B-300   Highly acclaimed hand-held antitank weapon produced by Israel Military Industries and soon to be issued to IDF infantry and paratroop units as a replacement for the RPG-7. The B-300 consists of a bazooka-like launcher and an 82mm rocket able to penetrate 550mm of steel armor. The B-300 combines the most reliable and practical properties of both the American 66mm LAW and the RPG. At the time of this writing, the U.S. Marine Corps has ordered 180,000 B-300s!

Beretta M1951   A 9mm automatic pistol built under license in Israel, and one of the most popular sidearms in use.

CAR-15   The short-barreled version of the U.S. M-16 5.56mm assault rifle, modified in some instances by the IDF Ordnance Corps to carry the

The ubiquitous GALIL assault rifle goes everywhere with the IDF soldier.

A paratroop sniper improves his mark on a firing range with his M-21 sniper rifle.

130

M/203 40mm grenade launcher. It is the favored weapon of most IDF combat unit officers.

FN MAG Belgian 7.62mm light machine gun produced under license in Israel. The mainstay squad support IDF weapon for well over a generation, the FN MAG has seen action from the liberation of Jerusalem in 1967 to the siege of Beirut in 1982. Reports indicate that the IDF plans to phase out the FN MAG in exchange for its lighter 5.56mm-caliber counterpart the Mini-MAG, much to the delight of soldiers who found carrying the FN MAG, at 24 pounds plus, a hefty chore.

GALIL 5.56mm family of assault rifles produced by Israel Military Industries since the mid-1970s. The GALIL combined the most effective qualities of the AK-47 and the M-16 into a comprehensive weapon system with three variants: the GALIL ARM with built-in bipod, a GALIL AR (without bipod), and short-barreled GLILON SAR, which has also been modified to carry the M203 40mm grenade launcher.

LAW Light antitank weapon. American 66mm anti-tank rocket in widespread use in all IDF combat units.

M-14/21 American 7.62mm rifle accurized into a sniper's weapon.

M-16 The ubiquitous American 5.56mm assault rifle, issued in the mid-1970s as a stopgap weapon while the GALIL was in production, and now issued to rear and Women's Corps units.

M-26 Fragmentation hand grenade produced by Israel Military Industries.

MAPATZ TOW antitank guided weapon (ATGW) modified to be portable and crew carried, with improved electronics by Israel Military Industries. It is guided by a laser beam and able to penetrate 800mm of steel armor.

RPG-7 Extremely effective Russian antitank rocket captured in such vast quantities that it became a standard issue item to paratroop, infantry, and combat engineer units.

In Hebrew, it's pronounced "TOH." Paratroopers prepare to demonstrate just how accurate their American-made ATGW is.

UZI Undoubtedly the most famous weapon ever produced in Israel. The lightweight and uniquely designed 9mm submachine gun entered IDF service in 1955 and soon became *the* symbol of the Israeli soldier. Although used extensively during the 1967 Six Day War, the 1967–70 War of Attrition, and the 1973 War, the UZI's limited range warranted it being phased out of front line service. Today, the UZI is produced in many variants, including a mini-UZI and UZI pistol, and is the favored weapon in countless nations. In IDF service, however, it is found only in the hands of reservists and female soldiers assigned garrison duty.

ARMORED FIGHTING VEHICLES

BATA'SHIT A modified and heavily armed command car used for joint-security duty along the frontiers.

131

Centurion MBT (SHO'T) British main battle tank which entered IDF service in the early 1960s, and armed with the lethal 105mm main armament, proved its worth as the master of the battlefield in both the 1967 and 1973 wars. Today, almost forty years after the first Centurions were produced, the SHO'T (Whip) has been modified and equipped with Blazer reactive armor for front line combat service well into the next century.

M109AL The IDF's premier artillery piece. The American 155mm self-propelled gun entered widespread service in the "dark days" following the

The IDF Armor Corps's version of the "Charge of the Light Brigade" on the sands of the Negev Desert — MERKAVAS, with M113s trailing faithfully behind.

1973 Yom Kippur War. It was extremely effective during the 1982 invasion of Lebanon as both a long-range artillery piece and a devastating short-range weapon.

M113 Known affectionately as the Zelda, the ubiquitous armored personnel carrier is the IDF's premier transport vehicle with over 4,000 in service. Like all foreign-produced weapons systems that

132

have reached Israeli hands, it has been heavily modified and improved, including add-on plates of armor.

M163 Vulcan   20mm self-propelled antiaircraft gun mounted on an M113 chassis. Issued to the Israeli Air Force, the Vulcans proved their worth during the Lebanon fighting as a viable deterrent to Syrian antitank helicopters, and as a brutally effective ground support weapon against Palestinian fortifications.

MERKAVA   Considered by many to be the finest main battle tank in the world, the MERKAVA was conceived as a result of Israel's battlefield experience and sensitivity to casualties. With a unique low slope design, and the engine placed up front, the MERKAVA is one of the safest tanks in the world, and with its 105mm gun, one of the most lethal. Its baptism under fire was in Lebanon, where it proved supreme.

Patton (MA'G'AH)   The American Patton series of MBTs (M48 and M60) began arriving in Israel in the mid-1960s and were subsequently up-gunned and re-armored, being the ideal recipient of the Blazer reactive armor blocks.

T-54/55 and T-62   Soviet MBTs captured by the IDF in substantial quantities from the Egyptians, Syrians, and Palestinians since 1967. In IDF service, they have been up-gunned, equipped with new engines and Blazer armor, and are known as the TIRAN. Their cramped conditions, typical of Soviet tanks, made them highly unpopular vehicles to serve in, and they are not reported to be in front line service.

Morning in the Negev Desert. Tank crews, mechanized infantry formations, artillery batteries, and combat engineers prepare for division-size maneuvers.

Jonathan Torgovnik, IDF *Spokesman*

About the Author

Samuel M. Katz was born in 1963 and served in the Israel Defense Forces at the height of Israel's involvement in Lebanon. He has had a life-time interest in Israeli military matters and has written over a dozen books and articles on the subject, including *Arab Armies of the Middle East Wars, Israeli Tank Battles,* and *Follow Me: A History of Israel's Military Elite*. Katz has recently completed *Guards without Frontiers,* a study of Israel's war against terrorism, and is currently at work on a POWER title for Presidio Press on the Israeli Air Force, and an in-depth history of Israeli military intelligence.